HITTING TOWN
AND
CITY SUGAR

Hitting Town opens with Ralph, [obscured by barcode sticker] from Birmingham University, dropping in unexpectedly on his sister, Clare, in her Leicester bed-sit. Together they decide to 'hit the town'. But against a background of commercial radio, city-centre-precincts, Wimpy Bars and dangerous practical jokes, the incestuous relationship that develops between them seems the only way of affirming their vitality . . .

City Sugar, a companion piece, focuses on Leonard Brazil, the local disc-jockey heard briefly in the first play, as he dispenses milk chocolate pap over the Leicester air-waves. The worlds of commercial radio and teeny-boppers collide with the mounting of the grotesque Competition of the Century, into which Brazil pours all his self-hatred and his contempt for his Miss Average Listener.

With these two plays, Stephen Poliakoff won the 1975 Evening Standard 'Most Promising Playwright' award.

Hitting Town was first seen at the Bush Theatre, London, in April 1975, before touring the country and playing at the Edinburgh Festival. A television version was shown in 1976, starring Mick Ford and Deborah Norton. *City Sugar* also seen first at the Bush, opened in the West End with Adam Faith in the lead in March 1976.

'Stephen Poliakoff's new play, *Hitting Town,* strikes me as a stupendous achievement . . . *City Sugar* marks the most exciting and auspicious West End debut for a generation.'
Frank Marcus, *Sunday Telegraph*

'Stephen Poliakoff's *City Sugar* is a savage dissection of that pristine slagheap of Our Times — mass culture . . . Poliakoff has neatly concertinaed black comedy and social realism and it is not to be missed.'
Ann McFerran, *Time Out*

'A scathingly brilliant play . . . Simply by concentrating on the essentials, Mr Poliakoff produces a world of technological nightmare.'
Irving Wardle, *The Times*, on *City Sugar*

by the same author

In Methuen's New Theatrescripts
STRAWBERRY FIELDS

Stephen Poliakoff

Hitting Town
and
City Sugar

EYRE METHUEN · LONDON

First published in Methuen New Theatrescripts
in 1976 by Eyre Methuen Ltd, 11 New Fetter Lane,
London EC4P 4EE
First published in this revised edition as a Methuen Modern Play
1978
Copyright © 1976, 1978 by Stephen Poliakoff
Music and lyrics of *Yellow Blues* and *I Can Give You Love*
copyright © 1976 by Hugh Thomas
ISBN 0 413 38880 8

CAUTION
All rights whatsoever in these plays are strictly reserved and
application for performance etc. should be made to Margaret
Ramsay Ltd, 14a Goodwin's Court, London WC2. No
performance may be given unless a licence has been obtained.

Set IBM by 𝕬 Tek-Art, Croydon, Surrey.
Printed in Great Britain by Cox & Wyman Ltd.,
Fakenham, Norfolk.

To Karin

HITTING TOWN

Hitting Town was first staged at the Bush Theatre, Shepherd's Bush, London, in April 1975, with the following cast:

CLARE	Judy Monahan
RALPH	James Aubrey
NICOLA	Lynne Miller

Directed by Tim Fywell

It was subsequently televised by Thames Television on 17 April 1976, with the following cast:

CLARE	Deborah Norton
RALPH	Mick Ford
NICOLA	Lynne Miller

Directed by Peter Gill
Produced by Barry Hanson

The action takes place in a city in the Midlands, e.g. Leicester.

The set should be suggestive of an overall precinct-style environment, neon lit, in which Clare's room is the dominant part, a featureless nasty blank box. Other areas and the front stage can be used for the rest of the locations — walkway, precinct, snack bar, and disco — which can be suggested simply by concrete blocks etc., litter bins, and bright striking graffiti.

Characters
RALPH. He is twenty, messy appearance, attractive and with considerable nervous charm. His energy is a mixture of a sharp humour and a dangerous vulnerability.

CLARE. She is thirty and seems old for her age. Very efficient but withdrawn manner, but extremely poised and seemingly in control.

NICOLA. She is sixteen. Totally flat voice, but a very determined manner underneath the quiet, completely blank exterior.

Author's Note
RALPH and CLARE hardly ever see each other as is evident from the first scene. It is important that their tone to each other in the opening moments of the play is totally and only that of elder sister to a highly troublesome younger brother.

Scene One

Blackout. Voices on the telephone.

CLARE. Who is this? (*Pause.*) Who is this speaking?

RALPH (*with a foreign accent*). Hello.

CLARE (*impatient, loud*). WHO is this?

A dim spot comes up on CLARE *talking at the sort of telephone box found on landings.*

RALPH (*accent*). Want to ask you about your knickers, lady. I mean are they the see-through variety. Can one see through them — if one looks . . .

Silence.

CLARE. Oh, it's you. (*Pause.*) Where are you then?

RALPH (*normal voice, terse*). In a phone box.

CLARE. Are you still in Birmingham?

Pause.

RALPH. No. I'm by the station.

CLARE. So you're here at last.

RALPH. Maybe.

CLARE (*annoyed*). I thought you said you'd be here by lunch-time.

RALPH. Well I wasn't, was I?

CLARE. You really shouldn't be so unreliable, you know. I never thought you'd be as late as this. (*Pause.*) You coming now?

RALPH. Probably.

CLARE. Well I'll see you soon then, won't I? (*She replaces the receiver loudly.*)

RALPH (*as she does it*). Could be.

Lights up full on the room area. CLARE's *room is a bare wooden box — modern, hideous, with a door leading to a bedroom off.* CLARE *is tidying brusquely, slightly bad tempered; she is about 30 — withdrawn, efficient appearance.*

RALPH *stands in the doorway; he is 20, untidy, unshaven. Both are nervous, but offhand.*

RALPH. I'm here.

CLARE. So I see.

RALPH. Good.

CLARE. You're late.

RALPH. I apologise. (*Leaning against the door, chewing, his manner is unexpected, edgy, but light.*)

CLARE. What you chewing?

RALPH (*continuing to chew*). Nothing. (*He puts his hand up to his mouth, slips something out of his mouth into his pocket, moves past her.*)

CLARE. Are you all right?

RALPH. Yes, tremendous. (*He moves into the room.*) I can't stay long.

CLARE. You look a mess.

RALPH. Do I? I got wet on the train.

CLARE. On the train?

RALPH. Yes, it rained. All the time. (*He looks down at his feet.*) And it got in.

CLARE. You haven't got a hole in your shoes.

RALPH. No, I don't think so. Only a small opening.

CLARE. Why do you let yourself look like that?

RALPH. Like what? (*Slightly aggressive.*) I look fine — people stop me in the street and tell me so. (*He moves round the room — slight smile, edgy. Suddenly.*) Tell you something, on the train there were two people making love on the lavatory. No, honestly, this is true. It's not uncommon now. And the whole carriage was listening. We couldn't help it — we could hear the noise. All of us pretending to ignore it, reading our newspapers as it grew louder.

CLARE. Really.

RALPH. Yes — really. (*He sits on the bench-type sofa. Pause.*) You'd believe anything. I think I'll have a quick nap now. IF I may.

CLARE (*surprised*). Now?

RALPH. You know, sleep.

CLARE. Where?

RALPH (*lying down*). Here'll do. (*He snuggles down with his coat still on, as she watches.*) You don't mind, do you?

Silence. His eyes shut.

CLARE (*looking down at him, sharp*). You might take your coat off first.

Lights fade to blackout.
Immediate but slow fade up.

RALPH (*just before the fade up is complete*). Am I awake? (*Pause.*) How long have I been asleep?

CLARE. About two minutes.

RALPH. Oh Christ — (*He turns over.*) — I couldn't think where I was. (*Pause. He curls up again.*) You've grown fatter you know.

CLARE. Thanks.

RALPH (*curled up*). My pleasure.

CLARE (*quiet*). I went through a compulsive eating stage for a bit. Had to have the feel of food in my mouth all the time.

RALPH (*loud, not listening to her*). What's that noise? (*He sits up suddenly, staring at the back wall.*) Sssh.

CLARE. There's no noise.

RALPH. I heard something. (*He lies down again, curls up.*)

CLARE. How's the architecture going?

RALPH (*curled up, grunts*). All right.

CLARE. Have you been doing any work then?'

RALPH. Why — should I have been?

CLARE. I was worried about you, you know.

RALPH. Were you — why?

CLARE. You know why. The bombings.

RALPH. Where? What bombings?

CLARE. In Birmingham.

RALPH. Those bombings.

CLARE. Yes, those. I thought you might have been near them. (*Pause.*) Were you?

RALPH. No. (*He shifts his position, turns his back.*) I'm here aren't I?

CLARE (*watching him*). You've got to ring mother.

RALPH (*quiet*). Yes. (*Suddenly loud, sitting bolt upright.*) For chrissake. It's getting *louder!* — the noise. I'm trying to go to sleep for Godsake. Don't people realize?

CLARE. What noise?

RALPH. You must be able to hear it. (*He points to the wall.*) From there. Noise. It's late — he shouldn't be making noise. Who lives there?

CLARE. I don't know. I've never ever seen him.

RALPH (*turning*). You've never seen him!

CLARE. He doesn't come out. Must be nervous.

RALPH. It definitely has got louder! How come you can't hear it?

CLARE. I can just. It's always on.

RALPH. Do you wear ear plugs then?

CLARE. Occasionally.

RALPH. It's not a very pretty picture that. You curled up here, your ears stuffed with ear plugs. (*Facetious smile.*) Are they very big? Can I see them?

CLARE. You're putting mud all over the floor you realize. If you're going to be a nuisance you can leave.

RALPH. Right.

CLARE (*snapping*). And take that coat off for Godsake.

Silence. RALPH *watches her, puts the thing back in his mouth, lies down, chewing.*

RALPH. I got your letter.

CLARE. Did you?

RALPH. It was full of moans.

CLARE (*gets up*). Was it?

Pause.

RALPH (*moves his head, stares up at her*). How are you then?

CLARE. I manage . . . more than manage.

RALPH. Then why did you write to me?

CLARE (*suddenly looks at him*). I don't know. Because I haven't seen you for five months.

RALPH. You never usually write to me.

CLARE. No. (*Pause.*) I'm beginning to wish I hadn't. And stop chewing that . . .

She moves past him — he puts out a hand, catches hold of the beads round her neck.

RALPH. What's that?

CLARE. It's mine — and I like it.

RALPH (*looking at her dress*). And is this one of your firm's — wearing your own products are you?

CLARE. Yes. An old one.

RALPH. It's hideous. (*She moves away.*) Why've you had your phone removed?

CLARE. I just didn't want it in here. I was getting dirty phone calls too. (*She glances at him.*) Like yours just now.

RALPH. That wasn't very dirty — you're a bit isolated, aren't you really.

CLARE. Lonely you mean.

RALPH. Yes.

CLARE. Then say it. I'm not anyway.

RALPH. Do you miss him?

CLARE. Not much.

RALPH. Then cheer up.

CLARE (*quiet*). I'm all right.

RALPH (*suddenly, very loudly*). GO ON, CHEER UP! (*He hits the floor hard, but not aggressively.*)

CLARE. Don't.

RALPH. Why not?

CLARE. You're making me sound like a depressed menopausal old hag. (*She turns.*) Am I?

RALPH. No. (*Slight smile.*) Not menopausal. (*He is still chewing away.*)

CLARE (*staring straight at him*). Thank you.

RALPH. You're still quite attractive.

CLARE. What do you mean still?

RALPH. Still. In a way.

CLARE (*looking up*). What you got in your mouth, Ralph?

RALPH (*chewing*). Nothing.

CLARE. Come here. Come on — what is it?

RALPH. Nothing special. (*Slopping loudly*). An old penny I found on the platform.

CLARE. You didn't. You are disgusting.

RALPH. I've had it in my mouth the whole journey. Tastes rather nice, quite powerful.

CLARE. Take it out. Come on.

RALPH *spits the coin into his hands.*

RALPH. Actually it's only a new coin. You should try it sometime.

CLARE. You could have poisoned yourself.

RALPH (*slight smile*) Do I get a sisterly kiss now?

CLARE. Not in that state you don't. Do you ever change your clothes?

RALPH. Of course.

CLARE. You need to be put through a mangle probably, several times. Why you looking at me like that?

RALPH. Because I was. (*He lights a cigarette.*)

CLARE. I thought you said you'd given up smoking.

RALPH. I have. (*He takes a drag.*) Till this evening. (*He swings round.*) Anyway there're cigarette burns all the way round here.

CLARE. I do that sometimes.

RALPH. It looks as if you've been trying to burn yourself out of here. Doesn't it!

CLARE. Well I haven't.

RALPH. Are things as bad as that?

CLARE (*staring straight at him*). No.

The noise from next door is growing louder.

RALPH (*suddenly swinging round*). Listen! No — ssh — (*Loud.*) Listen! It's getting even louder.

CLARE. He may be waiting for his request to come up.

RALPH (*with sudden energy*). Probably sitting there in a totally bare room, in a high chair. A little scabby man, in black leather and yellow socks, with a streaming nose and a bald head. Do you think!

CLARE (*watching him, slight smile*). Maybe.

The music is getting louder.

RALPH. Oh Christ! This is ridiculous! Can't even hear ourselves speak. (*He suddenly turns and hammers on the wall, incredibly loud.*) Turn it down. Quiet! Down!

Silence. RALPH *turns, smiling.*

There. That's the way to do it.

The music starts again.

CLARE (*looking at him*). Not much good are you?

RALPH. I've only just started. Haven't I. (*He moves up to her.*)

CLARE. What's the matter?

RALPH. Nothing. (*He looks at her.*) Do you want to come out for a meal with me.

CLARE. Is that an invitation?

RALPH. If you like.

CLARE. All right, I will.

RALPH (*moving to go.*) Right then.

CLARE *turns, goes over to the wardrobe, takes clothes out. Her back to* RALPH, *she pulls her top off, bare-backed, moves off-stage to the bedroom.* RALPH *gives a quick glance towards her, as she goes, then turns away, moving about the room.*

RALPH. This is just a box you know. Really badly made — terrible finish. Cheap and nasty. (*He stops, crouches down.*) And look at this. Lots of dead insects here.

CLARE. What?

RALPH. Insects. A whole pile of them here.

CLARE (*calling*). Yes. They get in there. Behind the wood somehow. Get trapped in the night. I hear them knocking themselves out.

RALPH (*standing up with some in his hand*). I've got an idea, Clare.

CLARE. What's that?

RALPH. To shut up our friend. (*He kicks the wall.*) Go up to his door you see, and feed these through the crack. Flick them under the door — so they come at him. Terrifying.

CLARE (*coming back into the room, authoritative*). No, you don't.

RALPH. Why not?

CLARE. Come here, Ralph, give those to me.

RALPH. No.

CLARE. Give those here.

RALPH (*loudly*). Come on — are you ready? (*He moves towards the door.*)

CLARE (*trying to grab insects*). Ralph.

RALPH. Careful, you'll squash them.

CLARE. Look, I'm not having you being childish. (*He moves on to the landing. She follows.*) Leave those here. (*Lowering her voice.*) And sssh — you can't be a menace out here, please . . .

RALPH. It won't take a moment.

CLARE (*loud*) Give those beetles to me Ralph.

RALPH. It will work.

CLARE (*very loud*). I said HAND OVER THOSE BEETLES. (*She giggles, suddenly, then stops herself.*)

RALPH (*drops the lot, then starts*). Hey! one of them was alive! (*Loud.*) You didn't tell me one of them was alive. (*Silence.*) You look quite nice, you know.

CLARE (*sharp*). We're paying compliments now are we?

RALPH (*raising his voice, so the whole building can hear*). BUT DO YOUR ZIP UP.

CLARE (*looking down, embarrassed*). It's not undone, Ralph.

RALPH. Don't argue. Do your zip up lady. You're indecent like that.

CLARE (*hissing*). Stop it. You'll get me a bad name.

RALPH (*even louder*). Just do it up a little further. You're nearly there.

   CLARE *is backing away.*

CLARE. You're embarrassing me, you know, Ralph.

RALPH. Good.

   Blackout.

Scene Two

The walkway, suggested by a concrete shelf. Behind it the wall is covered in graffiti — of all sorts.
RALPH *is moving about holding a Coca-Cola can.* CLARE *is sitting, drinking through a straw.*

RALPH. GET DRINKING. Go on.

CLARE. I am.

RALPH (*slight smile*). Is this a good start to your evening?

CLARE (*sucking the straw*). Not very, no. (*She looks about her.*) I don't especially like walkways, least of all at night.

RALPH. Why not? (*Facetious smile.*) What's wrong with them? (*He moves up to her, quieter.*) Anyway you've got to enjoy yourself. (*He looks at her.*) You haven't been out for ages, have you?

CLARE. I have.

RALPH. Not properly. Not for a really good time.

CLARE. No. (*He is staring at her.*) Ralph — why do you keep on looking at me like that?

RALPH. Do I?

CLARE. You know you are. Never seen you stare so much at anything.

RALPH. Am I? (*Pause.*) Can't think why I am. (*Quiet, coolly.*) You've been looking at me, haven't you?

CLARE. Not much.

RALPH. I haven't seen you for a long time. Just refreshing my memory I expect . . . (*He swings round.*) Great place now, isn't it? All this new stuff round here. Fantastically well planned.

Pause.

Our home town. (*Loud.*) Get drinking!

CLARE. You haven't started yours.

RALPH (*holding his can over the flame of her lighter*). No — I'm heating mine.

CLARE. Heating it.

RALPH. Yes, to make it warm. To show you something when it's really hot.

CLARE (*beginning to get nervous*). What'll happen?

RALPH. You'll see in a moment. (*He turns the can over in the flame.*) Come on — get hot.

CLARE. What are you doing Ralph? (*She stands up.*) Is that going to do anything? You'll frighten people you realize.

RALPH (*staring at the lighter, turning the can round*). Could be.

CLARE. One can't go anywhere with you, can one, without you . . . causing trouble.

RALPH. Right now, we'll see.

He puts the can down several feet in front of him.

(*Smiling broadly.*) Keep your eyes fixed on that. It's only small . . . but when I pour your ice cold drink over it, it should . . .

CLARE (*getting up, backing away*). No, stop it . . . please.

RALPH. Where are you going? Ready. Watch!

CLARE *backs away.* RALPH *with a very sudden movement pours her drink over his can.*

Silence.

CLARE *stares fascinated at the upright can.*

RALPH. You see. Absolutely nothing. (*He tosses the can loudly at her, smiling.*)

CLARE. For chrissake, I was about to block my ears! You're an idiot!

Pause.

(*Looking at him.*) It's totally unsafe to be with you, isn't it?

RALPH. Of course.

CLARE (*slight smile*). I'm here at my own risk, I suppose.

RALPH (*looking up at her*). That's right.

CLARE (*slight smile again*). I ought'to be insured — shouldn't I?

Silence.

RALPH (*suddenly stops gazing at her, looks at the ground*). Clare . . . look I don't know quite how to put this but . . .

CLARE (*sharp*). Put what?

RALPH. This . . . (*He looks at her, then away.*) It's quite funny . . . but I keep . . . I keep on — (*Slight smile.*) — Christ! . . . Do you know what I'm going to say?

CLARE (*avoiding his eyes*). No.

RALPH (*glancing at her*). Don't you . . . (*Nervous laugh.*) No. Then forget it.

CLARE. What?

RALPH (*jumping up*). Sssh — there're people coming. (*He moves over towards the wall.*) Be quiet. Sssh.

CLARE. What on earth's the matter?

RALPH. No they're gone — you can stop worrying. (*He swings round.*) Have you seen all this — (*Staring at the graffiti-covered wall.*) Some real British Graffiti — see what he says . . .

(*He looks at it, reads*). 'Even the Queen enjoys it' . . . Yes . . . 'City rules OK' . . . 'Red Killers' — who do you think they are? (*Staring right up to the wall.*) You can learn a lot from this wall. Some of it is very fresh too. Newly done. The paint's still wet. (*He pulls his hand down the wall, smudging the paint; he grins at her.*) Some fresh graffiti, Clare.

CLARE (*slight smile*). Yes.

RALPH. And really fiercely written too, see. Jagged writing. We must have just missed them, by a few seconds . . . whoever did it! (*Putting the palm of his hand on the wall and smiling.*) Think of people standing up here scribbling away with anything they can get hold of. Pouring it all out. Everything's here!

CLARE (*watching him*). Just kids with nothing else to do.

RALPH (*gazing straight at her*). That's right. So give me a pen now.

CLARE. Oh no you don't.

RALPH. Give me a pen.

CLARE. It's against the law, defacement.

RALPH. That' s a lie for a start. This is a public graffiti spot. Purposely put here to encourage it, let things get out. It's reserved for it. So give me that pen.

CLARE. It says 'Prohibited' up there.

RALPH. That's out of date. Give it here!

CLARE (*hesitates, then throws the pen*). You shouldn't.

RALPH (*catching pen*). That's better. (*He writes in red in huge letters. R A L P H.*) And now through the middle. (*He draws a huge 'C' through the middle.*) That's you. (*She moves up to him. RALPH faces her.*) Ralph was here with C.

Pause. He smiles.

So now you're equally guilty.

CLARE (*catching hold of him, slight smile*). Why you so excited Ralph, tell me.

RALPH. Why shouldn't I be — it's allowed. Anyway I'm not at all. I'm perfectly calm. (*He smiles.*) Does it make you nervous!

CLARE (*slight smile.*) A little.

RALPH. That's all right then.

Muzak begins to play.

Listen! The Sound of Muzak. (*He moves.*) We ought to follow it. (*He turns, touches her.*) Don't worry Clare, you're going to have the time of your life. (*He moves again, CLARE catches hold of him.*)

CLARE (*looking at him*). You've got to phone our mother, remember.

Blackout.

Scene Three

In the blackout we hear the voice of LEONARD BRAZIL, *the local disc jockey, loud, authoritative, brash.*

L.B.'s VOICE. Hello there. This is LS — who else — YOUR LOCAL SOUND. And this is Len-Don't-Switch-Off-Brazil on night call saying this is your line all the way through to midnight. This is LS on 55304, that's 55304. So night callers everywhere let's hear those phone's ringing . . . as . . . from . . . now!

Muzak comes up — the sort played in a restaurant — and lights up on a Wimpy, where CLARE *and* RALPH *are sitting at a table, no food, only one side plate. Just behind them and to the left is* NICOLA *in her waitress uniform, sitting eating. She is 18 years old. The Muzak goes on playing, but quietly.*

RALPH (*quiet, in public*). This is ridiculous. (*Pause.*) This is ridiculous Clare.

CLARE. They'll come eventually.

RALPH. What do you mean, eventually? They haven't even looked at us since we arrived.

CLARE. Probably think we're here for the music.

RALPH. It's all planned. They keep you waiting for as long as possible to lower your resistance, part of their national policy. (*He looks about him.*) Look at it! Think of the people that never eat anywhere else. (*He looks at her*). I want you to have quite a nice meal.

CLARE. Thank you.

RALPH (*still quietly, but with feeling*). God I hate these places. They're multiplying all the time. Must make millions every day. They ought to be hounded.

CLARE (*smiling, leaning towards him*). Being the rebellious student now are we, continuing your college activities . . .

RALPH *glances towards her with a slight aggressive smile. Then he turns.*

RALPH. Over here! (*He waves his arm.*) Could we have our food. (*Pause. Stronger.*) Please could we have our food. (*He turns back.*) It'll come now.

CLARE. It better.

Muzak playing.

RALPH. Or else what'll you do?

CLARE (*leaning towards him*). Make you listen to this for the rest of your short life.

RALPH. We will anyway. There's no escape. (*Louder.*) There's one woman, you know, one *single, anonymous, lady,* who arranges all this muzak, produces it, by herself, she does, this is true! It just pours out of her, uncontrollably, tons and tons of it! A real madwoman.

CLARE (*watching him*). Really.

RALPH. There are three enormous warehouses of it. This is absolutely true. And they take it away in lorries — tankers . . . Drive it to every corner of England. Everywhere you go you hear her artistry, flowing out. She can rise both to a small cafe and a major airport. The lot. To keep the people 'happy'! And you know something. She lives in this town. Here. She does.

CLARE (*touches him for a second*). Really?

RALPH. We ought to find her, quickly, she's contaminating the whole place.

CLARE *brushes some ash off the table.* RALPH *catches hold of her hand.*

And stop doing that can't you? You're always tidying. It's a dreadful habit.

CLARE. Listen, Ralph, you're not going to make an exhibition of yourself now.

RALPH. NO!

CLARE. Do you hear. You're taking me out. And God I'm hungry.

RALPH. Really hungry.

CLARE. Yes.

RALPH. OK then, we'll make our own food.

He takes some brown sauce, begins to squeeze it out onto the side plate.

CLARE. What? Look, I told you a moment ago . . .

RALPH. No don't worry, this tastes quite good. In fact it's better than what they give you. There's plenty here for both of us.

CLARE. You're being childish now, aren't you?

RALPH (*looking up, loud*). Look will you stop telling me to stop being childish. (*Silence.*) Now do you want to eat something or not?

CLARE. Yes, but —

RALPH. Right, now watch. You put this on first. (*He finishes with the brown sauce.*) Then two portions of this unflavoured mustard. (*He dollops them on.*) Then half a packet of crisps going blue at the edges that I happen to have ready prepared. This is about the only food you can get round here any more. (*Loud.*) And by God it's good.

CLARE. Ralph . . . she's watching us.

RALPH (*not looking up*). Is she? She can have some too. This should be enough. (*He puts the crisps away. Fast.*) Then take anything else you have in your pocket, like old sweets, tobacco or nougat, I've saved a piece of Mars bar. (*He cuts it, squashes it in.*) And throw in a few tranquillisers.

He pulls them out of his pocket and drops the pills in.

CLARE. What you got tranquillisers for, Ralph?

RALPH. Why not? They're for you. Stir the whole revolting mess together — (*He does so vigorously and aggressively.*) — and squidge it. You needn't worry, I've done this before. (*He adds vinegar.*)

RALPH *tastes it with his finger.*

Yes; now give me the tomato.

CLARE (*smile*). Look . . . (*She picks up a plastic, tomato-shaped sauce container.*)

RALPH. Come on, quickly — not there, in the middle. (*He puts it in the middle of the plate.*)

CLARE (*slight smile*). I see.

RALPH. Good. (*Pushing it towards her.*) Now you carve.

CLARE (*astonished*). Carve?

RALPH. Yes. Go on. People forget how good these things are.

CLARE (*smiles*). Don't be stupid.

RALPH (*louder, aggressive*). Look, how long have you been here.

CLARE. Half an hour.

RALPH. Then carve it!

CLARE (*picking up a fork and knife, hesitates*). All right — what — like this . . .

RALPH. Yes, go on. It comes open.

CLARE (*shoving her fork into the plastic tomato very hard*). Bloody thing! She's staring at us now!

RALPH (*looking at the waitress, who is staring*). No, she's not. Come on. More attack.

CLARE *drives the fork into the tomato hard.*

CLARE. You sure it comes open.

RALPH. Go on hurt it, more . . . it'll split open. You can do it.

CLARE. No. I can't. (*She pushes it towards him.*) Made enough of a fool of myself.

RALPH (*grins*). Have you? (*He picks up the tomato.*) We've got to see what's inside anyway. We'll open it this way. (*He unscrews the top.*) Yes — there we are. (*He pulls things out of the top.*) Bit of chewing gum — half of a sardine . . . lots of cigarette butts — (*He puts them on the table.*) — and what's this? (*He pulls something else out.*) And a tooth!

CLARE (*turns away*). Oh Christ . . .

RALPH (*wiping sauce off the tooth*). A big one. (*He puts it on the table.*) About what I expected.

CLARE. Did you.

RALPH. More or less. (*Smiling.*) You know each tomato will contain something different. Seriously! You can always tell a town by what's in its tomatoes. All its undesirables are pushed there. It spews out of them. (*He squashes the tomato.*) I'll have a look around. Collect the lot. (*He gets up.*) You'll learn a great deal. See the whole revolting truth. (*He stands up*.) Shall I?

He moves across to the waitress.

Excuse me, can I borrow your tomato?

NICOLA (*looking up from her food*). What?

RALPH. Thanks very much. (*He puts it down, smiles excitedly.*) We need some more, four at least.

CLARE (*catching hold of him*). That's enough Ralph . . . enough.

RALPH (*sitting*). Is it?

CLARE. Yes. (*Slight smile.*) If I was to leave you alone for five minutes you'd cause complete chaos, wouldn't you.

RALPH. Am I embarrassing you then?

CLARE. No — you're not. But you're trying hard enough — aren't you.

RALPH. Could be.

CLARE. Well, you can give up, you understand.

RALPH. Can I?

CLARE. Because you won't succeed any more.

RALPH *moves slightly towards her, stops.*

RALPH. You're quite a tough customer, aren't you.

CLARE. Yes.

RALPH (*trying to throw her, smiling, broadly*). Are you thinking what I'm thinking.

CLARE. I don't think so . . . No, I'm not.

RALPH. Then you know what I mean.

CLARE. No I don't.

RALPH. Forget it.

CLARE. All right — I will.

RALPH *looks away* — CLARE *continues to look at him.*

Come here, you've got tomato on your lip. In fact it's all over your face.

RALPH. I know.

CLARE. Come here then.

RALPH *grins, tries to move away as she wipes it. She stops him, wipes his mouth for a moment, then kisses him.*

They kiss.

Complete silence. Silence held.

RALPH (*quiet*). That was all right.

CLARE (*very quiet, looking at the plate*). Yuh.

Pause. She looks at the waitress.

RALPH. She didn't see.

CLARE. Didn't she —

Pause.

Look I think . . . we better not ask questions, OK . . . Just . . . it happened. (*She puts the tomato back.*) Don't know what's got into us really.

RALPH. I knew you'd say that.

CLARE (*nervous*). Did you . . . (*Nervous laugh.*) You realize I'm known round here. I . . .

Pause.

RALPH (*suddenly loud*). Christ — they're still playing the same tune! How long have we been here?

CLARE. Thirty-five minutes — I don't know.

RALPH (*very loud*). Thirty-five minutes. Do you hear that? Look I know this is asking a lot. But could I have one glass of water. Just one glass of your water. We'll pay for it. A good price!

CLARE (*quieter, excited*). Stop showing off — do you hear!

RALPH. I'm not.

CLARE. Oh yes you are — incredibly.

She catches hold of him, sexual kiss, Silence.

Both sit still.

CLARE (*very quiet*). All right I . . .

RALPH (*not looking at her, squeezing brown sauce on to the tomato, very quiet.*) Quite exciting, isn't it?

CLARE. Is it? (*She turns, then turns back.*) Christ, she's seen us now. She has.

RALPH. Yes. (*He looks up for a moment.*)

CLARE. I think we better leave, hadn't we.

RALPH (*jumping up suddenly*). Of course. (*He moves towards the waitress.*)

CLARE. Where are you going?

RALPH (*by the waitress*). Here's your tomato back, thank you.

NICOLA (*pushing her plate away*). Yuh.

RALPH (*suddenly very loud*). Are you going to get us anything to eat?

NICOLA. I'm off duty, sir.

RALPH. But we haven't had anything to eat!

CLARE. Ralph. (*She goes up to them.*) Sorry we made such a mess on your table. We were just doing a little cooking. (*To RALPH, very quiet.*) Come on.

RALPH (*looking at NICOLA*). Is she going to report us?

NICOLA. No sir, I've finished for the night.

RALPH. Here. (*He takes out a coin.*) That's for occupying two seats for half an hour in these pleasant surroundings. It's for you.

NICOLA *looks at the money.*

NICOLA (*quietly*). OK then — thanks.

RALPH. What's your name?

NICOLA. My name. (*Pause; she is putting on her coat.*) Nicola.

RALPH. That is a nice name.

CLARE. Ralph. (*Tugging at him. To the waitress.*) I'm sorry. We're a little confused after sitting here for so long.

NICOLA. That's OK.

RALPH. Can we give you a lift anywhere?

NICOLA. You got a car then?

RALPH. No, we haven't. (*He looks at CLARE.*) I don't think.

NICOLA (*slight smile, moving out*). Excuse me. (*She goes out into the precinct.*)

CLARE (*to RALPH*). Stop it . . .

RALPH. I know what I'm doing. She's the only one that saw us, isn't she. Hey, wait . . . Nicola.

He crosses out of the Wimpy, into the precinct, followed by CLARE.

Lights change.

Scene Four

The precinct. Neon light.
RALPH *following* NICOLA *from the restaurant area into the precinct.*

RALPH. Come here a moment. (NICOLA *hesitates, comes up to him.*) There you are, that's for not reporting us back there. (*Nervous.*) Take it. (*He gives her some more money.*)

NICOLA. What? What you giving me this for?

RALPH. I told you, for not reporting us.

CLARE. Ralph. (*She pulls at him, moves him away. In a hissed whisper.*) Look what on earth are you doing? You realise you're drawing attention to us.

RALPH. I'm not at all.

CLARE. You'll make her incredibly suspicious.

RALPH (*loud*). Rubbish! Why should me giving her money make her suspicious?

CLARE. You're going to keep calm, Ralph.

RALPH. Don't worry . . . there's absolutely nothing to worry about.

NICOLA *is undoing a chocolate flake;* RALPH *goes up to her.*

RALPH (*conspiratorial, but nervous*). Actually you see . . . We've been exchanging dangerous substances in there . . . me and her, highly illegal, see . . . you know what I mean.

NICOLA (*silent laugh, knowing he is joking*). Oh, I see . . . OK then.

CLARE. Ralph.

NICOLA *is sucking her chocolate flake centre stage.*

NICOLA. Are you two from London then?

CLARE. No we're not.

RALPH. She went there, but she came back. (*Glancing at* CLARE.) It didn't work.

NICOLA (*looking from one to the other*). Oh I thought you might have been.

RALPH. Sorry no! I've just come from Birmingham.

NICOLA (*eating her chocolate flake, matter-of-fact*). You were one of the ones blown up were you?

RALPH. That's right.

NICOLA (*still matter-of-fact*). Were you nearly.

RALPH (*slight smile*). Yes — very nearly.

NICOLA (*looking at him, slight smile*). Were you?

RALPH (*suddenly*). Hey — did I introduce you? I can't remember . . . this is my *sister* Clare.

CLARE. For Chrissake!

NICOLA (*looking at both of them*). What! Your sister.

RALPH. Yes. (*He glances at her.*) She designs dresses sort of. For a rubbishy firm. (*To* NICOLA.) My *sister* does. Come here. (*He catches hold of* CLARE.)

CLARE (*hissed*). Stop it, Ralph — (*Close up to him, hissed.*) We're forgetting it ever happened, *remember*.

RALPH (*loudly*). Right.

CLARE (*strong*). Please . . . (*Up close to him, quiet.*) You realize what we've done is illegal, don't you.

RALPH. Don't worry. (*He kisses her on the lips.*)

CLARE (*pushing him off*). Stop it. DON'T.

Silence.

RALPH (*to* NICOLA). There you are, you see.

Pause. NICOLA *is leaning against the wall with her chocolate.*

Look at her. Totally calm. Hasn't batted anything.

CLARE (*quiet*). Thank goodness. (*Putting her arm round* RALPH. *To* NICOLA.) She knows you're only my boyfriend . . .

A burglar alarm suddenly bursts out ringing.

RALPH (*swinging round*). What on earth's *that noise?*

CLARE. What?

RALPH. That. Ringing the whole time.

NICOLA. That's a burglar alarm.

RALPH (*loud*). Simply everywhere we go there's noise. We must really attract bells. Look! There it is. Up there, see it. Tiny pink box terrorising the neighbourhood.

NICOLA (*not looking up*). Yes — it's always going on.

RALPH. You know this precinct well do you?

NICOLA. Yes. I'm here every day.

RALPH (*smiling at her*). That's good. You see, Nicola, I'm giving my sister — over there — a night on the town.

NICOLA. Are you? (*She looks at* CLARE.) I see.

RALPH. And we want to have a really good time. You see she lost her dreadful boyfriend a few months ago. She's got to let her hair down. (*Smiles.*) You understand — all the way.

CLARE. What the hell . . . (*Moving towards* RALPH.) Look, please . . .

RALPH. It's all right! Nicola's going to keep an eye on us. (*Smiling at* NICOLA.) Aren't you?

NICOLA (*slight smile back*). Yes.

RALPH (*swings round*). Going to show us round the new appalling precinct, isn't she. Look at it! Totally unsafe, it'd burn like balsa wood. (*Aggressive.*) And full of TV shops, it's just a morgue for them.

NICOLA. Yes, I watch those often. You can stand in front of them for hours watching for free. Till the colours go funny and you feel sick.

RALPH (*to* NICOLA). Whole centre has changed — me and my *sister* used to know a different place. Imagine being locked in here, the rest of your life unable to get out. (*He turns back to* NICOLA.) You know most of the architects of this atrocity are probably in gaol or just about to be. But we're left with it! Something ought to be done.

CLARE (*coming up*). Stop teasing her, for Godsake.

RALPH. I'm not teasing her.

CLARE. Look, we got to be careful, Ralph.

RALPH. I am being careful.

CLARE. What do you mean? You keep on telling her the whole bloody time. (*She turns.*) And now she can hear everything we're saying!

RALPH. Don't worry, she's the only one that knows yet.

CLARE (*snaps*). What do you mean yet? (*Moving towards him.*) Look we don't want to corrupt her, do we?

RALPH. You're the only one that's been corrupted.

CLARE. Is that so?

RALPH. Yes. (*He smiles, touching her hair.*)

CLARE. That's what you think. (*Looking at him.*) You're totally irresponsible, do you know that, Ralph. (*Not looking at NICOLA, she hisses.*) Why doesn't she go away for heaven's sake. She keeps watching us.

RALPH. Because she's interested, isn't she. Look! She's finished her chocolate.

NICOLA. Yes.

RALPH (*going up to her, grinning*). You have one each evening.

NICOLA. That's right. (*Standing by the bin.*) Here — you can see all the ones I've had for weeks. They don't empty them much.

RALPH. Look Clare. You can see all her dead chocolate skins . . . What do you do all by yourself every night, apart from eating chocolate?

NICOLA. Nothing much. Why? (*To herself.*) Sometimes I shout.

RALPH. What?

NICOLA. Nothing.

RALPH. Sometimes you shout. Is that what you said?

NICOLA. Yeh. When it's empty like this.

RALPH. You shout very loudly?

NICOLA *nods.*

Do it now.

NICOLA. No . . . I couldn't.

RALPH *turns.*

NICOLA. Well . . . I

She moves forward. Her face is calm, expressionless. She lets out a sudden short scream. RALPH *turns. Silence.*

CLARE. What a horrible noise.

NICOLA. Something like that. Don't do it often.

CLARE. Look you better have a cigarette.

NICOLA. No thanks. I don't smoke.

CLARE. And you mustn't believe what he says.

LEN BRAZIL's *voice suddenly pipes up.*

L.B.'s VOICE. That was — (*Title of the music.*) — and this is Len Brazil on night call saying this is your spot. So don't forget folks. More calls please on 55304. Just pick up your phones, and stimulate us . . .

RALPH (*half way through L.B.'s speech*). Oh shut up, just shut up. Leave us alone. (*He lights a cigarette.*)

NICOLA. Your hand's shaking.

RALPH. Is it? Here have a cigarette, you need one.

CLARE. No — I just offered her one. She doesn't smoke.

RALPH. Rubbish — here take one quick.

NICOLA. No thanks.

RALPH. Come on, take one. (*Loud.*) Go on — take the bloody thing!

CLARE (*loud*). Look everyone calm down. (*Really loud.*) JUST CALM DOWN FOR CHRISSAKE.

Silence. Distant Muzak. NICOLA *is leaning against the wall between them.*

NICOLA. Are you *really* brother and sister?

They look at her.

NICOLA (*to* CLARE). I mean are you his sister?

CLARE (*totally thrown*). Me? Oh Christ . . . No, of course not.

NICOLA (*to* RALPH). Are you her brother?

RALPH. Yes — of course I am.

NICOLA (*grins*). I see.

CLARE (*loud*). You've told her now.

RALPH. I'd told her before.

CLARE. But it's for real this time. (*Suddenly loud.*) Why don't you tell everyone. Go on. Put an ad in the local paper. (*Indicating the precinct speakers.*) Why not broadcast it over the loudspeakers.

RALPH. OK I will, shall I.

CLARE (*startled*). What do you mean?

RALPH. Phone him up.

CLARE. Who?

RALPH. The disc jockey. The phone-in. Shall I? (*Over by the phone.*) Why not? It's what they want on their shows, isn't it.

CLARE. Ralph . . . Christ . . .

She leans back as RALPH *picks up the phone. She covers her ears in embarrassment, but is smiling.*

RALPH (*disguising his voice*). Hello, is that the phone-in. I want to speak to Mr Brazil, please. Yes, on this is your spot. Can I please . . . Yes . . . 54203. Jeremy . . . Thank you very much indeed, that's very exciting. (*He puts the phone down.*) They're going to ring back.

CLARE. I thought you were going to do it for a moment.

RALPH. I might.

CLARE. Will you? I don't think so. You're a great one for suggesting things.

RALPH. Am I?

NICOLA (*moving over*). You going to speak to Len Brazil.

RALPH. Yes.

NICOLA. Ah. I tried ringing him once. Didn't get him. He never rang back.

RALPH. He won't ring back now.

NICOLA *begins to move off.*

Where you going now, Nicola.

NICOLA. Going down to the disco.

RALPH (*smiles, moving towards her*). The disco.

NICOLA. Yeh, it's my night tonight, my spot.

RALPH. You got all your friends there.

NICOLA. My friends.

RALPH. Yes.

NICOLA. Yeah . . . a few. It's all right there. Some nights. If you're lucky. Bit of a squash.

RALPH. Better than this place.

NICOLA (*quiet*). Yes.

RALPH. Right then.

> *The phone rings loudly.*

Oh Christ! That can't be him, can it?

CLARE (*turning, smiling*). Won't be anybody else, will it.

RALPH. No. (*He is stranded centre stage.*)

> *Pause.*

CLARE (*loud*). Well, go ahead and do it. If you're going to do it.

RALPH. Shall I?

CLARE. Don't just talk about it. (*He picks up the phone.*) Go on!

LEONARD BRAZIL's VOICE. Hello. Hello, caller.

RALPH. Hello . . . (*Putting on his small boy's voice.*) I want to speak to Leonard Brazil.

L.B.'s VOICE. Go ahead please. Leonard here.

NICOLA. You've got him.

L.B.'s VOICE. What's your name please.

RALPH. Jeremy.

L.B.'s VOICE. Hello Jeremy.

RALPH. I want to ask you something, Leonard.

L.B.'s VOICE. Fine, go ahead. This is your spot. How old are you Jeremy?

RALPH. Eleven.

L.B.'s VOICE. Eleven — near your bedtime isn't it, Jeremy, getting close anyway —

RALPH. I've got a sister.

L.B''s VOICE. Fine Jeremy. That's very good. What's her name?

RALPH. Lucy.

L.B.'s VOICE. Fine . . . Jeremy. That's good. Ask your question — THIS IS YOUR SPOT, night callers everywhere, pick up your phones, for a direct line on to LS and your host — as always — Leonard Brazil. Let's hear your views and blues all the way through to midnight.

RALPH. Well it's about me and my sister.

L.B.'s VOICE. Is she in the telephone box with you Jeremy?

RALPH. Yes — she's right by me, Leonard.

L.B.'s VOICE. Put her on the line, Jeremy, let's say hello to her.

RALPH. Christ — Here.

CLARE (*taking the phone, speaking in her ordinary voice, not young but quiet*). Hello there Leonard.

L.B.'s VOICE. Hello, Lucy. Speak up can you. They're a lot of people listening. How old are you Lucy.

CLARE. Eleven.

L.B.'s VOICE. You're eleven too . . . Tell me Lucy, are you twins, you and Jeremy?

CLARE. No — we're not.

L.B.'s VOICE. Fine, very good. Well it's near your bedtime too. Nice to talk to you Lucy. Can you put Jeremy back on the line, just hand him the receiver.

NICOLA *snatches the receiver.*

NICOLA. Hello Leonard — this is your spot.

L.B.'s VOICE. Are you there Jeremy?

RALPH. Yes, I'm here Leonard.

L.B.'s VOICE. I thought we'd lost each other for a moment. Go ahead Jeremy, ask your question — Three minutes to news time on LS.

RALPH. Well Mr Leonard, me and my sister we just gone to bed together.

L.B.'s VOICE. Hold it there, Jeremy. You're sleeping in the same bed with Lucy. Is it a double bed or have your mother and daddy got guests?

RALPH. No — you see we've just done sex together, my sister and me, sexual inter —

L.B.'s VOICE. Christ. Abort. I said abort. What's happened — have we aborted?

RALPH (*normal voice*). You'd better abort bloody quickly.

L.B.'s VOICE (*really angry*). So you're still on the line you little shit. How old are you really?

RALPH. Twenty-one.

L.B.'s VOICE. Are we off the air yet? — This is Leonard Brazil, this is your spot. (*Muzak comes on.*) So you're twenty-one years old Jeremy. You think this is a funny joke to play on the listeners.

RALPH. It's not a joke — Mr Brazil.

L.B.'s VOICE. Well, let me tell you, we have a lot of people ringing up on this programme with genuine problems. (*Loud.*) I said genuine problems. Don't you ring off yet, I haven't finished with you — just hold on to your receiver if you can, and listen to this Jeremy. (*Getting really worked up.*) We're off the air now, you creep and I'm telling you it's because of shits like you that we have trouble and violence in this city. And now I'm going to tell you something Jeremy which probably nobody's had the courage to tell you before —

RALPH *hangs up. Silence.*

RALPH. We done it.

CLARE. Not bad. You lied a bit.

RALPH. Yes. But we're famous.

Blackout.

In the blackout. LEN BRAZIL's *voice, confident, authoritative, slightly threatening.*

L.B.'s VOICE. Yes — I just want to say to all those upset callers we've heard from, that these people were obviously very sick and very stupid — practical jokers. And the sort of people that you and me can easily do without. It's what gives phone-ins a bad name, this sort of filth going out on the air. There're some very nasty customers even in a city like this, but luckily they're pretty few and far between. And I can tell you, we're not in the least afraid to take action against them. If they try to be clever again, we'll trace them, and have them dealt with accordingly. So rest assured. (*In his normal voice.*) And now let's change the mood . . .

Scene Five

Blackout. Music loud. Dancing bubblegum music. In the disco.
NICOLA *leaning against the wall.*
RALPH *and* CLARE *just a little in front of her.* RALPH
dancing − CLARE *moving more restrainedly.*
The music dips for a moment.

DISC JOCKEY's VOICE (*loud, trying to sound transatlantic*).
   GET DANCING!

   The music continues but quieter. RALPH *moves towards*
   CLARE.

CLARE (*warning*). Don't come too close, Ralph.

   RALPH *is closing up.*

RALPH. I'm not.

CLARE. You are. (*She glances over her shoulder as she moves.*)
   It may be my imagination but isn't absolutely everybody
   looking at us.

RALPH (*slight grin*). I should think they are. (*He looks round
   silently.*) Not many of them are dancing − just standing.

CLARE. We're something for them to stare at, aren't we. Wonder
   what they're thinking. (*Pause. She moves, grins nervously.*)
   God knows what I'm doing here. Haven't been to a place like
   this for years!

RALPH. You look good. (*Moving closer.*) Quite different. You
   realize the whole town will be talking about us soon. You'll
   have to learn to live with it. By morning we will have caused
   a sensation Clare.

CLARE. What you mean? (*She looks up.*) What you expecting?

RALPH. Your guess is as good as mine.

CLARE (*strong*). No, it's better. (*She drinks out of a bottle from the side. With a slight smile.*) We're regressing the whole time, falling backwards, soon we'll be aged three, you realize and have wetted our beds. (*She drinks again.*) It's way past my bedtime.

RALPH (*up really close*). No it's not, you're going to let your hair down, remember.

DJ's VOICE. That was — (*Title of the song.*) — and now here's a really smoochy number for all you smoochers to have a little smooch to. So get to it quietly, as the bishop said to the actress. Whoops, what am I saying. (*He starts the smooching music.*)

RALPH *moves up to* CLARE.

CLARE (*firm, warning*). Stop it!

RALPH (*turning to* NICOLA). This disc jockey's tongue's made out of foam rubber, isn't it. (*He turns.*) God, this is a nasty sight.

NICOLA. It's always like this. Each Sunday. It's all right here.

RALPH (*looking round at* NICOLA). Look, one filthy black room as small and squashed as you can get. Hell on earth. If anything went wrong we'd all be done for — never get out. And the heat, Nicola — it's difficult to breathe.

NICOLA. Yes — it gets like that.

RALPH. The only place you've got to come to! And the kids aren't even dancing.

NICOLA. They don't feel like it.

RALPH. They all look as if they've got glass eyes don't they. Totally glazed . . . (*He looks at them.*) Limp.

NICOLA. Excuse me — got to get ready — it's my night tonight. (*She takes out a box with glitter make-up in it.*)

RALPH (*turning, looking at her, smiles*). You ought to get away from here, Nicola. Leave town. You're too good for this place. (*Louder.*) I mean what are you doing stuck in this mad hole a hundred feet below a multi-storey car park. Being ordered what to do. (*Smiling at her.*) By total morons.

NICOLA (*smiles*). Yes.

RALPH. Who probably loathe your guts.

He turns, moves forward, suddenly grinning, putting on manager's voice, upper class.

Hello! Good evening. Hold it there please. (*The music stops.*) Nobody move. Just wanted to introduce myself — here I am — and wish you a pleasant evening on behalf of the management. And so, feel at home, let — it — all — hang — out for as long as possible and spend very freely. That's what we recommend.

DJ's VOICE. Hello there! I think we have a little trouble over in the corner. Come out of there you slinky corner huggers and GET DANCING.

The music starts again.

CLARE. You're going to get us into trouble you realize.

RALPH (*smiling broadly*). We are in trouble, already.

CLARE (*slight smile*). And you'd make it worse, wouldn't you, given half a chance. (*She picks up her bottle again.*) I'm going to get really drunk tonight, anyway, if I'm not allowed to go to bed.

RALPH (*smiling*). You are going to bed eventually.

CLARE (*warning*) You're coming too near. I said not to. (*Suddenly she shouts very loudly.*) GET OFF!

Pause. RALPH *glances startled over his shoulder.*

RALPH. All right then. (*He moves straight over to* NICOLA, *with a seductive smile.*) What you waiting for Nicola?

NICOLA. My spot. It's coming soon. (*Slight smile.*) I've had to wait weeks.

RALPH. Your spot. (*He smiles.*) I see. (*Coming very close to her.*) You don't know what it's like having a relationship with one's sister, do you. It's a tricky business, I can tell you. Can be explosive, as you've seen. (*He touches her.*) Or perhaps you do know . . . you got a brother?

NICOLA. Sort of.

RALPH (*smiling, touching her*). Sort of. I see, and what's he like then.

NICOLA. Don't see him very much, now.

RALPH. Don't you? Why not, Nicola? (*He touches her lightly, nervous laugh.*) Perhaps you should meet him, soon.

CLARE (*suddenly moving over to him, loud*). What you doing with her?

RALPH. Nothing.

CLARE. What disgusting suggestions was he making? (*Slight smile.*) Been making up to you, has he?

NICOLA (*slight smile*). Not really.

RALPH. No!

CLARE. He's a total menace. Can't be left alone with anybody for two minutes without trying something. You have to fight back. (*Looking at the glitter make-up.*) Shall I help you with that?

NICOLA. I can do it myself, really.

CLARE (*close up to her*). I'll do it. You want to look very striking, don't you. (*She touches* NICOLA's *dress.*) You're wearing one of our bad dresses — an old one. Where do you want these? All over.

NICOLA *nods.*

(*Looking at the glitter.*) You got a lot here haven't you? (*She looks at* RALPH.) What on earth's she going to do?

RALPH. I have no idea! Here, you better have some of this. (*He lifts the bottle up to* NICOLA's *face.*)

NICOLA. I don't drink. Not usually.

RALPH. Come on! (*He puts the bottle up to her lips.*)

CLARE. She's quite calm.

NICOLA *hands the bottle back, her face very serious.*

NICOLA. I've got to take my shoes off too.

CLARE (*brushing* NICOLA's *hair, smiling*). You're going to look good Nicola. Really outrageous! Magnificent in fact — like nothing they've ever seen. And very, very sexy! You want to, don't you. (*She puts some glitter on* NICOLA's *face. As she does so.*) To think I wasn't even allowed to walk barefoot round the house at your age, let alone not wear a bra, and look like you. (*She looks at her warmly.*) But you're not much better off are you, really. You don't look that happy, do you?

NICOLA (*matter-of-fact*). I'm all right . . . It's very soon now.

CLARE (*putting the glitter on*). God, she's pale isn't she. Like some night creature.

RALPH. She probably hasn't seen daylight for weeks. Been living off strip-lighting hasn't she — like you.

He touches CLARE.

CLARE (*slight smile*). Keep your hands to yourself, I warn you. (*Very close to* NICOLA.) You ought to get away from here Nicky, you know.

RALPH (*smiling at* NICOLA). You see.

CLARE. Your face is finished anyway.

They stare at her.

Doesn't she look *good.*

RALPH. Yes.

NICOLA (*staring back*). Are you *really* brother and sister? I mean . . . after . . . tonight. Are you?

CLARE. What do you think?

NICOLA. I don't know.

Pause.

What does he do then?

CLARE. He's a student, isn't he. (*She touches* RALPH's *arm for a moment.*) A total idler — a waste of money.

RALPH. A usual grey, turgid student —

CLARE. Who doesn't believe in anything.

NICOLA (*quiet, staring at them*). No, I mean — what does he do to you?

CLARE. Nothing — we don't ask questions like that. You've to forget all about us, forget our faces.

RALPH. Yes.

NICOLA (*staring straight at them*). I mean, does he touch you and things . . . and . . .

CLARE. Don't be vulgar. Of course not. Don't worry.

NICOLA. Maybe he will.

CLARE. Don't be stupid. He knows better than that, doesn't he?

RALPH. Oh yes! (*He puts the bottle to* NICOLA's *mouth.*)

CLARE. Sssh — you're making her nervous.

RALPH (*grinning*). You're the one that's nervous.

CLARE. Rubbish! (*Trying to take the bottle.*) And give that to me!

RALPH (*smiling, teasing*). No. I think you've had enough don't you.

CLARE. Come on. (*Very loud.*) GIVE ME THAT BOTTLE RALPH.

NICOLA. Excuse me. (*Moving between them.*)

The music stops.

It's my turn now.

DJ's VOICE. And now, we hand over to you. For a moment. Is tonight's lady ready? — Whoever she is? Tonight . . . the brave girl is . . . er . . . Nicola Davies. Good for her. — Of 35 Poole's Road. So let's all give her a chance now.

NICOLA (*moving into the spotlight, she picks up the microphone*). Good evening — it's my turn now. (*She holds the microphone up to her mouth.*) OK — ready. (*She is really concentrating; her face is totally calm, expressionless.*)

The taped music starts; she starts singing along with it, then loses it. The tape stops.

(*Quiet, calm.*) OK, start it again please.

RALPH (*loud*). Go on, sock it to them Nicola!

NICOLA *throws back her head nervously. Her face is totally expressionless, then she launches into* Wheels on Fire — *singing along with the actual tape which is playing quietly. Her concentration is total, her expression remains completely blank, but we feel something building up inside her, a clenched feeling, and during the second verse she gets louder and louder, until after the last line of the verse, a tremendous and shattering scream comes out of that calm face and we feel real danger. The tape cuts out.*

NICOLA (*total blank stare*). Thank you.

Blackout.

Scene Six

Blackout. A voice.

VOICE. Efforts are being made to trace the two voices purporting
to be children who caused a sensation over the air a few
hours ago.

The lights start coming up. We see it is RALPH speaking.

They made lewd and outrageous suggestions to the compere,
one Leonard Brazil, and claimed to be indulging in incestuous
practice. They are still at large and could prove extremely
dangerous. (RALPH *is leaning against the door of the room.*)

CLARE. You ought to ring your mother.

RALPH. Our mother.

CLARE. You gotta do it. One phone call, that's all she likes.

RALPH (*staring at her*). It's too late now, isn't it.

CLARE *is turning away.*

She never says anything anyway.

CLARE. God. I'm full of drink. It'll slop out. (*She swings round.*)
What are you doing?

RALPH. Only taking my coat off.

CLARE. Yes. Good. So where are you going to sleep then?

RALPH. I don't know. (*He stares at the sofa.*) Down there.

CLARE. Yes. It's the only place.

(*She turns, sudden.*) God, I hate this room. Do you know
that. I really detest it. I do. What can one do in it. It's a
wooden cell. I'm always banging and cutting myself on things.
You get room sores from this building . . . you know . . . I
got them all over me.

RALPH (*quiet*). Have you? I can imagine, yes . . .

CLARE *looks up, catches his eye, turns away.*

CLARE. I haven't been up this late for months, years even. I'm
always in bed.

RALPH. Doing what?

CLARE (*half turns*). Awake. (*Slight smile.*) By myself. Listening
to the kids downstairs knocking about in the car park,
smashing and screaming. I can never sleep.

RALPH. Remember Nicola. (*He opens his mouth in a silent shout.*) I don't sleep much either now. (*Watching her.*) What you doing?

CLARE (*with her back to him, taking rings off her hands slowly*). Taking these off.

RALPH (*nervous*). Yes. You'll probably get a dirty phone call in a moment. It's undoubtedly the little man next door. It's the only way he can talk to you — sweaty phone calls. He's bound to have a spy hole in this wall — (*Running hand over it.*) — and he watches as you take your things off. All your neighbours have them probably, one there — (*He points.*) — one there, and one directly above. And they watch you . . . like a rat in a cage. They may be watching us now.

Silence.

You're a long time taking those off.

CLARE (*still with her back to him*). Am I?

RALPH. Yes you are. And you're standing like that on purpose, aren't you?

CLARE. Like how?

RALPH. Like that — now.

CLARE. Why?

RALPH (*loud*). I don't know.

Pause.

Have you had lots of men?

CLARE. Men? A few. Not so many. (*Still with her back to him, brushing hair.*) How many have you had?

RALPH. Men —

CLARE. No. Start with the others.

RALPH. Three.

CLARE. Ever?

RALPH. Yes. That's the lot.

CLARE. More than I'd had at your age.

RALPH (*suddenly urgent*). *Clare* — What's the time? I said — WHAT'S THE TIME?

CLARE. I heard.

RALPH. Well answer.

CLARE. Don't shout.

RALPH. I'll shout if I like.

CLARE. I've no idea. Two, three? I've forgotten all about time now.

RALPH (*very loud*). You see! I don't believe it. Listen. (*Very loud.*) Listen to that!

Silence. Both listen. There is distant Muzak and a voice.

(*Very loud, excited.*) At this time! And it's still going on —

(*Moving over to the wall.*) Alone in his room. (*He suddenly shouts.*) Be quiet — or we're coming to get you.

He punches the wall savagely.

CLARE. Stop it — for Chrissake.

Pause.

RALPH. Clare . . . my hand's — gone through the wall.

CLARE. What you mean?

RALPH. It has. Look. (*He tries to pull it out, masking her view.*) I told you these walls were ridiculously thin! (*Loud, angry.*) They're like paper! (*He pulls.*)

And I can't get it out. It's gone all the way through —

CLARE (*quiet*). Oh God . . .

RALPH. It's sticking out the other side — right out. I can feel things . . . in the room. . . I can feel his bald head. I'm touching it now . . . and it's very rough . . . like sandpaper.

CLARE (*realizing*). Ralph!

RALPH *pulls his hand out from behind his body, really excited.*

RALPH. You believed me. You did. (*He shouts.*) You believed me!

CLARE (*moving over to him, excited*). Sssh. Just shut up. (*She shakes him.*) You'll have the whole building down here.

RALPH. What does it matter? (*He smiles at her.*) One ought to live dangerously.

CLARE (*slight smile*). Dangerously? (*Moving up to him.*) You're determined to get us caught aren't you?

RALPH (*nervous smile*). I'm not!

CLARE. You've already done enough to get us burnt, you realize, if this was another century.

RALPH (*loud*). Me! I have!

CLARE. Yes. You have! Except you probably wouldn't have burned. They'd have had to keep on relighting you.

RALPH. What's that meant to mean?

CLARE (*excited, close to him, but not loud*). What do you think?

Pause.

Come on, tell me, why are you like this?

RALPH. Like what?

CLARE (*prods him*). This . . . here.

(*With a provocative smile, touching him.*) You've given up all your rebellious activities . . . at college, haven't you.

RALPH. Yes b-

CLARE. You see.

RALPH (*fast, strong*). Because there's nothing going on anymore is there! . . . Except one or two people with tiny minds just in it for their careers.

CLARE (*loud*). Really? (*Smiling, moving up to him.*) Why are students now all so grey and defeated, and miserable and can't do anything? At your age . . . tell me? (*She is staring straight at him.*) You're almost incapable of action, do you know that?

RALPH. Really? And you were different were you?

CLARE. Oh yes. (*She smiles, pause.*) Haven't seen me like this, have you? (*Up close, quiet, touching him.*) Look at you, all that energy and you just don't know what to do with it, all you can do is thrash about and *shout.*

RALPH. Is that so.

CLARE. Yes — it's so. (*She smiles.*) You've always been like this, had energy. (*Matter-of-fact, not seductive.*) I remember taking a huge sticky bandage off you, once, when you were small, only time I touched you probably, and you were just beginning to have hairs on your legs, and I pulled it off really slowly, all the way down, and hurt you like nothing had ever before, and you . . . nearly tore the place down, a whole explosion, almost wrecked the entire house.

Pause.

(*Matter-of-fact.*) But you can't do anything with it.

RALPH (*smile*). We'll see.

Pause.

Are you feeling nervous too?

CLARE. About what?

RALPH (*nervous smile*). For Chrissake!

(*He moves away. Lightly.*) Christ . . . I wish that noise would stop. I really do. (*Facing her again.*) Just for a moment —

CLARE (*smiling*). You're very sensitive to noise aren't you — (*Suddenly more gently.*) Those bombs gave you a scare did they —

RALPH. No. (*Pause. He is looking at her. Lightly.*) You know what we ought to do, Clare, we ought to have one week of total terrible insanity together. When everything will suddenly cease to exist . . . you see — fade right away. We'd get into a car, with a gun maybe, and some music, and set off, just like any film. And probably have a few sudden killings, you know, in the hot sun on the motorway. Through windscreens. And keep moving all the time, be fired at from bridges, and be chased through some big city, and drive on until we were almost senseless, you see, and then get cornered, and caught, and shot several hundred times, very slowly. Coming?

Pause.

CLARE. What a useful idea.

RALPH. Yes. (*He takes his jacket off.*)

CLARE. What you doing now?

RALPH. Taking my jacket off.

Pause.

Want me to go any further, I mean.

CLARE. What did you say?

RALPH. You heard.

CLARE. Do you mean it?

RALPH. Mean what.

CLARE (*louder*). That . . . Do you mean it?

RALPH. Half . . . I mean . . .

CLARE (*quieter*). You ought to be careful what you say Ralph.

RALPH (*smiles*). I am.

CLARE. Well what were you trying to say.

RALPH. You know what I meant. I mean . . . (*He begins to giggle.*) FOR CHRISSAKE!

CLARE (*loud, but smiling*). Stop giggling and tell me. Go on. (*She moves forward.*) You think you can suggest things and then just draw back, don't you? But you can't you know, because it just doesn't work like that.

RALPH. No.

CLARE. You've always thought you could get away with every-thing haven't you — the spoilt little brother . . . (*Moving forward, loud.*) All the time — anything.

RALPH. I haven't always managed it. Because you've been around.

CLARE. Like now.

RALPH. Yes.

Pause.

All right then Clare.

CLARE (*loud*). What you mean — 'all right'?

RALPH (*smiles*). Come here.

CLARE. You really want to.

RALPH. Yes.

CLARE. You've made up your mind.

RALPH. Yes.

CLARE. That's a change. Good.

(*She casually strokes his hair then gives him a very sexual kiss.*) You're very cold. Why are you so cold? (*Looking at him*.) You've got the same bad complexion as I have — your skin — all spots. (*Touching him*.) You're really rough up here. And you're too thin. Much. (*Slight smile*.) I'll crush you flat probably.

RALPH. You won't you know.

CLARE (*quiet*). Are you clean then, everywhere?

RALPH. Of course I am.

CLARE. Let's have a look. (*She moves his head slightly*.) Not very, no. But you'll do. I think. (*She is staring straight at him*.) Won't you.

Blackout.

Scene Seven

Blackout.
Loud radio murmuring — half heard sounds, talking fast. Then the phone starts ringing. Very dark.
Long loud ring.
CLARE *comes out on to the landing, half dressed.*

CLARE. Oh Christ.

She stumbles about in the dark; the ringing continues.

Yes!

Pause. She grabs the phone. We hear on the line, occasionally, through the conversation, a female voice, only half audible, whining. No words are distinguishable, only her noise.

Hello! . . . Who is this?

Pause.

Look, who the hell is this?

Pause.

Mum — what on earth — do you know what time it is? . . . Oh. What do you want? No I wasn't asleep actually. I haven't been asleep at all. (*Slight nervous laugh*.) Christ! No, I didn't say anything. I . . . It's early morning . . . No, I've just been, I've . . . just . . . been occupied . . . All night . . . Yes . . . I . . .

RALPH *moves into the lighted area.*

No, I'm all right. Just hold on.

RALPH *moves closer.*

Here. There's someone to speak to you. (*She holds it out to him.*)

CLARE (*as RALPH takes it*). It's your mother.

RALPH (*disguising his voice*). Hello . . .

Pause.

Hello there . . . this is Paul. Yes — I'm a friend of your daughter's.

CLARE (*slight smile*). Stop it . . .

RALPH. Yes, this is Paul speaking. I've just become friends with your daughter. I . . . I've been keeping her company. For the night.

CLARE. Come on — we don't want to upset her.

RALPH. She's a nice girl your daughter. Very polite. (*He begins to giggle.*) Christ. No, listen . . .

He is giggling even more, almost hysterically. CLARE *begins to giggle too.*

(*To himself.*) Shut up! . . . (*He puts a hand over the receiver. Loud to himself.*) God, I can't stop it. (*Loud.*) Stop it.

He lifts the receiver.

Hello mother, actually, it's me. Me! It's not fuck, who did I say it was . . . No, it's Ralph. (*Shouts.*) RALPH!

He starts giggling all over again.

God I can't stop it. Hold on mum. I'm just — (*He bites his lip.*) No, I wasn't laughing — I was just coughing. Look I'm sorry I didn't phone before . . . I was going to but I didn't. I was busy . . . BUSY!

He bursts into helpless giggles — holds out the receiver to CLARE.

Look you take it. (*Loud.*) Take it, for Chrissake.

CLARE. No, you talk to her.

RALPH *drops the receiver. It hangs between them on the end of its flex.*

RALPH (*to* CLARE). Go on!

>(*The phone hangs there.*) Oh Christ — this is ridiculous. (*He picks up the receiver.*) Listen Mum. (*Very serious voice.*) It's difficult at the moment to talk. Difficult! (*To himself, as he feels he is going to giggle.*)

>Get a grip — stop it. (*Shouts.*) Oh shit!

>*He puts the receiver back on the rest with a loud thump in the heat of the moment, then he realizes.*

>Look . . . I've rung off now.

CLARE (*serious*). Pick it up, quick, she may still be there.

RALPH (*picking up the receiver*). Hello Mum — you there?

>*Pause.*

>I don't know if she's there or not. (*Loud.*) Mum? (*He lets go of the receiver.*) No, she's gone.

>*Silence.*

>She probably only wanted the holiday rent. (*Nervous smile.*) Her ringing now!

CLARE. You should have done it before. (*Quiet.*) She's gone anyway.

>*She is by the phone.*

RALPH (*swings round*). No, leave it off, I'll ring her later.

>CLARE *moves back into the room. Greyish white light, getting brighter.*

>(*Suddenly quiet.*) You know it's almost morning.

CLARE. It is morning. It's arrived.

RALPH (*astonished*). *Now.* Is it?

>*Pause. He is watching her.*

>Are you all right then?

CLARE. Me? I'm fine. Just cold.

RALPH. You realize we haven't slept at all. Aren't you exhausted?

CLARE. Not much.

RALPH (*nervous grin*). No, not at all. We'll probably start hallucinating from lack of sleep in a moment.

He bangs the wall with the palm of his hand.

CLARE (*swings round*). Sssh.

RALPH. What do you mean 'Sssh'. I can do that. It's time he was awake.

Pause. RALPH's manner is a mixture of nervousness and dangerous lightness.

It's terrifyingly quiet, isn't it, Clare.

CLARE. For once, yes.

RALPH. Quite eerie. (*He moves.*) It's a horrible light. We're very high up here aren't we . . . (*He looks at her.*) Do you think there'll be anything about us on the radio this morning. Should be.

He watches her.

(*Snaps.*) Why you getting dressed?

CLARE. Because I have to.

RALPH. You don't have to. There's no reason at all to. (*Lightly.*) We don't have to take any notice of morning. (*Slight smile.*) You're not getting ready for work anyway.

CLARE *continues to get ready.*

(RALPH *is watching her; his tone is light.*) Clare . . . you know it was really quite like this, when one of the bombs went off right outside, last week, you know.

CLARE (*with her back to him, quiet*). So you were near them. I thought you were.

RALPH. Yeh, I was. Right on top. All the glass was smashed everywhere. (*He watches her, his tone light, trying to get her attention.*) It's a funny feeling . . . I can tell you, afterwards . . . You know next day I expected every car I passed to go off. (*Smiles.*) I got this idea, rather crazy really, that when I was walking along the pavement if I stepped on the lines a steel mantrap would spring up and get me by the leg, right there — honestly. I was sweating, just walking along. (*He looks at her.*) And you know, the day before yesterday I saw a car parked. And I knew just like that it had a bomb in it, you see. It was a dirty green mini, vicious looking. Are you listening? — And I went up and leant against it, Clare, yes.

It was hot — the metal was — though the air was freezing. And I leant right on it. But nothing happened.

Pause. He continues, trying to get her to turn round.

You know something kicks into place in your mind after a loud bang, it does. The place . . . and things . . . comes into focus . . . everything one's thought. All the streets . . . and buildings begin to look, you know . . . dangerous, all of it. The whole hideous heap . . . Birmingham. You know what I mean? It's a real dump, Clare.

Pause.

You're very calm suddenly.

Pause.

You shouldn't be getting dressed. Did you hear what I said?

CLARE. Yes I heard.

RALPH (*loud*). Then don't.

CLARE. I'm doing what I want.

RALPH (*slight smile*). You're not even looking at me.

Pause.

Are you feeling guilty then?

CLARE. About what?

RALPH. Don't start that. You know what I mean. (*Pause.*) About us doing it — are you?

CLARE. Feeling guilty?

RALPH. Yes.

CLARE. No, not really. Why should I.

RALPH (*slight smile*). You haven't even mentioned it, have you.

CLARE. No.

RALPH. Come here. (*He catches hold of her, nervous smile, light.*) You don't think you're pregnant do you?

CLARE. Of course not.

RALPH. What would happen if you were. If you were really . . . I mean . . . how do you think the kid would turn out?

CLARE. There's no need to talk like that.

RALPH. It'd have an enormous head probably.

CLARE. I said don't.

RALPH (*slight smile*). No. (*He swings round.*) The noise is
beginning to come up, hear it?

CLARE. Yes.

RALPH (*quick smile*). Can't have that happening can we? Look
at it Clare. (*He half turns towards grey light.*) Great grey
mess — starting up again, spilling out. (*Quieter.*) I hate this
place now — this town! Quite a lot. Don't you?

CLARE (*matter-of-fact*). A little, yes.

RALPH. What you doing?

CLARE. Shivering.

RALPH (*moves up to her*). I'll stop it.

CLARE. No you won't.

RALPH (*slight facetious smile*). You don't want me.

CLARE. No.

RALPH (*grinning*). Why not? (*He moves away.*) So what are we
going to do about it all, Clare . . . We can't let it stay like
that. No. (*He tosses a coin, suddenly jokes. Fast.*) We could
throw something out of course, for a start. Drop this over, for
instance. Would probably make a hole in a traffic warden's
head. Right! (*He moves across.*)

CLARE. Stop it! That's dangerous.

RALPH *swings round.*

RALPH. That's better. (*He moves over.*) I don't like you too
calm. You've gone all quiet — (*He touches her face casually.*)
— and white.

CLARE. Do you want something to eat before you go?

RALPH. Before what?

CLARE. You go.

RALPH (*smiling*). Yes, I thought that's what you said. (*Tossing
up the coin.*) 'Before I go'. The only problem you see, is,
I'm not going back.

CLARE. Aren't you?

RALPH. No, you see, what's happening instead is — very simple. We're going off together. In a car, like I said. We can go by bus of course if you like. (*Slightly louder.*) But we're going to disappear anyway. Together, untraceable. Live in some very flat empty spot. (*Smiles.*) Marshy. (*Louder.*) That's what's going to happen you see.

CLARE (*slight smile, staring at him*). NO.

RALPH. What do you mean 'No'. It'll happen.

CLARE. I don't think so.

RALPH (*aggressive*). You don't think so. (*Then a broad smile.*) I thought you might agree. You want me to take myself off then, just like that.

CLARE. Yes.

RALPH (*staring at her, loud*). Right! (*He catches hold of her head, moves it towards morning light.*) You ought to look at it — (*Staring at her, with a slight aggressive smile.*) We're bigger than all of it you know . . . Yes. (*He turns, grins.*) I'm just going to make a quick call, OK.

CLARE. Who to?

RALPH. What do you mean who to? Just a call. (*He moves back to the phone.*) You stay there. (*He grabs the phone, moving very fast, flicks through the pages of a directory with the other hand.*) Getting very good at this aren't I. Very fast.

CLARE *is moving towards him.*

RALPH. No, you can stay there.

He dials, smiling broadly.

(*Adopting an Irish accent.*) Hello, is that the Mercury? Well listen to this will you. This is the IRA speaking.

He smiles at CLARE.

(*Loud.*) The IRA, you know —

CLARE. Ralph. (*She rushes onto landing area.*)

RALPH. Are you listening? I'm phoning a warning, you under-stand, and I will only say it once — Right! There's a bomb somewhere in the Haymarket.

CLARE (*loud*). What the hell do you think . . . (*She pulls at him. He fights her off.*)

RALPH (*very loud*). Did you hear that — I said a *bomb*. Christ this line is —

His voice begins to change.

And it's going off in ten minutes *flat*. (*He shouts down phone.*) Did you hear what I said?

CLARE. For Chrissake Ralph.

RALPH (*swinging round*). You keep out of this.

(*Loud.*) Hello, did you get that.

(*Raising his voice.*) Look you idiot you better get this bloody quickly.

CLARE. Ralph.

RALPH (*turning round*). Oh Christ. (*His voice at first under control.*) For fuck's sake — the pips are going . . . I've only just started. (*He pulls at the flex on the phone.*) What's this phone doing? (*He looks at* CLARE.) Come on quick, give me another 2p. (*Suddenly louder.*) Hurry! It's going wrong.

CLARE *doesn't move. Suddenly* RALPH *really shouts.*

I said give me another two pence. (*Really serious.*) Come on, RIGHT NOW. It's going to cut out. (*Beginning to sound dangerous.*) Did you hear what I said? . . . For fuck's sake. (*He moves, scrambles across the room, looking.*) It's going to cut out.

He stops scrambling, looks at her.

Why didn't you give me one. Didn't you hear me ask. DIDN'T YOU?

CLARE (*calm, but very quiet*). Yes.

RALPH (*screaming*). I asked you for one. I had them on the line. I asked you for one — you heard me.

CLARE (*quiet*). Stop it Ralph.

RALPH. If you'd given it me, I could have done it. Do you *realize that?* You idiot. You stood there. You didn't *even move!*

CLARE. I told you to stop it.

RALPH. And don't look at me like that.

CLARE. Are you going to control yourself?

RALPH (*suddenly screams*). I'm not going back! You heard me —
I'm not going. (*Shouts.*) I have no reason to go. None — *at all.*
And nothing you can do will make me.

CLARE. You're not scaring me one bit you know.

RALPH. There's nothing you can do you understand. (*Shouts.*)
And if you try!

CLARE. You're not a child, Ralph — stop it.

RALPH (*screaming again*). I am not *going back.*

CLARE. Come here.

She moves towards him.

RALPH. *I'm not.*

She catches hold of him.

Let go!

He tries to fight away.

You bloody keep off.

But she catches hold of him.

(*Quieter.*) Keep — off.

CLARE. Are you going to stop it by yourself? Or will I have to
make you.

RALPH (*quieter*). Try — go on.

CLARE *catches his head and pulls it downwards, they fight
for a long moment, he pulls away.*

Silence. RALPH *is pale but quiet.*

CLARE (*matter-of-fact*). You really shouldn't have done that
you know, Ralph.

RALPH. Shouldn't I.

Pause.

It was something wasn't it — (*Aggressive.*) — and you didn't
expect it . . .

Pause.

You could have got hurt you know.

CLARE (*staring straight at him, matter-of-fact*). You would have hurt me would you.

RALPH. Probably.

CLARE. But you didn't, did you.

RALPH. No. But very nearly. (*He moves slightly.*) It was something anyway. Would have been quite funny if it had worked.

CLARE. Would it? You'd have only got a few sirens going. (*Slight smile.*) That's not very much is it? And you'd probably have got gaoled.

RALPH. Yes . . . Maybe (*Aggressive.*) Saved by the pips wasn't I?

Pause. He looks up.

I'm thirsty Clare.

CLARE. Are you?

She passes him a bottle.

There.

RALPH *takes the bottle, takes a long drink.*

CLARE. Are you all right, Ralph?

RALPH. I'm fine. I am.

CLARE. It's not going to erupt again.

RALPH. Not for the moment.

CLARE. Good. You can catch an early train then can't you.

RALPH. Yuh — of course. The earliest you like.

(*Suddenly.*) Oh Christ — listen to that racket now.

We hear the rumble of the city.

It comes up quickly.

CLARE. It always does.

RALPH (*he glances at her*). Well, will you be wanting to see me again. I mean . . . you know.

CLARE. Yes, if you pull yourself together.

RALPH. Don't talk to me like that —

Pause.

CLARE. If you do . . . It might even happen again. I mean us. If we wanted.

RALPH. Yuh . . .sometime . . . maybe.

CLARE. Could even be soon, if you liked. It might be worth it. (*Pause. Slight smile.*) I wouldn't mind seeing you. It's up to you.

RALPH. Yuh.

CLARE. You know where to find me . . . You can come anytime.

RALPH. Yuh . . . Just ring . . . I know.

CLARE. And I'm often in.

RALPH. Yuh . . . maybe . . . sometime.

LEONARD BRAZIL *is heard, loud and clear.*

L.B.'s VOICE. Hello early risers wherever you are, it's three minutes to *seven o'clock*. Here's a bit of gentle rise and shine on the LB show. And if we can't have shine then at least we can have . . . (*He fades in some loud Muzak.*)

The Muzak goes on playing.

RALPH (*flicks the lighter, holds his hand over the flame; quiet, slow, with a slight smile.*) He's made of plastic and if I light this under him, he'll bubble and melt into a long black sticky line and flow completely away — taking all the rest with him.

CLARE. Yes.

She picks up the bottle.

When this music stops . . . I'm going to work.

She takes a long drink from the bottle.

Fade.

CITY SUGAR

City Sugar was first staged at the Bush Theatre, Shepherd's Bush, London on 9 October 1975, with the following cast:

LEONARD BRAZIL	John Shrapnel
REX	Leon Vitali
NICOLA DAVIES	Lynne Miller
SUSAN	Natasha Pyne
BIG JOHN	James Beattie
JANE	Hilary Gasson

Directed by Hugh Thomas

The play, in the revised version printed here, was subsequently presented by Michael White at the Comedy Theatre, London on 4 March 1976, with the following cast:

LEONARD BRAZIL	Adam Faith
REX	James Aubrey
NICOLA DAVIES	Lynne Miller
SUSAN	Natasha Pyne
BIG JOHN	Alan Hay
JANE	Hilary Gasson
MICK	Michael Tarn

Directed by Hugh Thomas

The action takes place in a sound studio of Leicester Sound, a local commercial radio station; in the Leicester branch of British Home Stores or Liptons (frozen foods counter); and in Nicola's bedroom in Leicester.

The time is the present.

Characters

LEONARD: in his middle to late thirties, extremely polished appearance, but dresses stylishly rather than ultra-fashionably, considerable natural charm, even when being aggressive.

REX: twenty-one years old, a mixture of eager awkwardness and cockiness. He has a likeable naive manner.

NICOLA: sixteen years old. Totally flat voice, but a very determined manner underneath the quiet, completely blank exterior.

SUSAN: is also sixteen, extremely volatile, attractive manner, with a lot of highly charged violence inside her.

BIG JOHN: small shiny man, in his late fifties, totally accepting manner; tidy, neat, completely dedicated to his job.

JANE: sixteen years old, quite a sharp competitive manner, but also nervous, and completely overcome by her surroundings.

MICK: shy seventeen-year-old, overjoyed to be working where he is.

Author's Note

It is important that Leonard's style as a disc-jockey is not too transatlantic, but his own special blend of relaxed charm, sudden fluent bursts of energy, and barbed comment. He is totally in control of his medium, and his actions round his desk and controls should suggest a master disc-jockey.

The tension inside him which explodes later in the play should build up gradually, both on and off the microphone — his considerable charm in the first scene, both to his audience and to Rex, getting progressively more and more sour, until eventually it becomes savage.

However, he never allows himself to over-step the mark *completely* when he is on the air, even in his huge speech at the end of the first act.

ACT ONE

Scene One

The studio. LEONARD BRAZIL *is sitting at the record desk.*
REX *is in the engineer's box. A pop record fades over a blackout.*

LEONARD (*into the mike*). From 1968, there, Amen Corner,
featuring the unmistakable soprano of Mr Andre Fairweather-
Low, and 'If Paradise Was Half As Nice'. Welcome back to
the LB show . . . LB — the two most important initials in the
country. LB on five hundred and fifty waves — that's a lot of
water. (*Loud.*) *Five hundred and fifty* medium waves!
(*Smiles.*) Sorry. 'You can do better than that, Brazil.' 'Yes
Boss.' In a few minutes we have something for you, something
special. (*Beginning to open letters on the turn-table desk.*) I
want to say hello to those I met in North Street yesterday;
people out in their gardens with *Green* fingers, very definitely,
and green feet too, so I'm told. And one even with green
hair. No, it was very nice meeting you. They have lovely
gardens up there, don't they, lovely houses! (*In his more
normal voice.*) I have a few letters in front of me — I've been
struggling to open. I have one from Mrs Lee, Mrs D. Lee,
saying that did I know there was now a topless restaurant in
this fine city of ours, and its name is the Aubergine — how's
that for a free commercial, you guys over there in the
Aubergine — and Mrs Lee wonders, what do I think about it?
I think — it's a very classy name, *'The Aubergine'*, perhaps
in French it is something more than just a vegetable. I wonder,
since we're being blue — or blue*ish,* perhaps we could ask —
would any of the ladies like to see bottomless waiters
approaching you with your curry? Rex is suggesting a lot
of rude vegetable jokes about what that restaurant would be
called, which I will ignore. Enough of this smut . . . I went to
the cinema yesterday, saw the very excellent *Death Wish,*
a lot of rape and gore and blood and guts, for those of you
that like your toast buttered that way — me, I prefer the
lovely, the scintillating, the mind-expanding Lynsey De Paul.
(*Over the beginning of the record, which he has switched on.*)
Nobody need fear — Lynsey De Paul is here . . .

He turns a switch, after a few bars so that the music now plays silently while the record goes round; he drops his biro onto the desk.

Pause.

LEONARD. That was execrable. (*He flicks the intercom to speak to* REX *in the box.*) That was a real stinker. A loosener — and a very loose loosener at that. (*Pause. He continues to the intercom.*) Come in here . . . It's the sleepy time for them at the moment, all gorged after Sunday lunch, lying in heaps round the room . . . they won't want to be stirred. (*Pause. Louder into the intercom.*) Get yourself in here, right now!

REX *enters behind him.*

REX. I'm here.

LEONARD. That's better.

REX. I've brought a drink.

LEONARD. How kind . . . (*Slight smile.*) Trying to placate me are you? . . . What is it?

REX. Lime juice; it's a free sample of one of the commercials we're carrying this week. I thought you'd like to try it.

LEONARD. It looks like a congealed shampoo. (*He puts it to one side. Suddenly staring at* REX; *loud.*) Now, why haven't you filled these up?

REX. I was going to.

LEONARD. Going to! Everybody keeps on telling me how efficient you are, how fortunate I am to have you. I have yet to notice. Go and do these now. (*Hands him sheets of record titles to be filled in.*) I warn you, it's a particularly grisly lot. (*Smiles.*) I seem to have played pap for an entire week — might as well have stuck the stylus into cotton wool. (REX *moves slightly.*) And why hasn't my mail been checked . . .

REX (*embarrassed*). Sorry, I . . .

LEONARD (*holding up letter*). I've been asked to open another municipal pleasure pond — which is completely out of the question of course.

REX. Why?

LEONARD (*rifling through his other letters*). The last time — the one and only time I had to baptise a pond — it was in front

of councillors and crowds, and all the rest . . . and I had to
launch it — with a champagne bottle, containing — (*Suddenly
looking up*.) — and this is completely and utterly true —
frog's spawn. A bottleful. I wasn't allowed to smash it against
the side of course, I had to solemnly pour it out, and of course
the bloody stuff got stuck and I had to stand there shaking it,
and banging the bottom, like a ketchup bottle, until of
course I got it all over myself. (*Looks up*.) What I really hate
is somebody that doesn't believe a good true story. (*Loud*.)
Get on with it! (REX *moves slightly. Loud*.) What's more, I've
never seen a single person even *near* that pond — thousands
of pounds spent on a small windswept hole in completely the
wrong place.

REX. I . . . By the way — I've left an item there — (*He indicates
the desk.*) — you might like.

LEONARD. You have, have you. Worse and worse, Rex . . .
You're having a good day, aren't you? (*Smiles.*) I don't like
suggestions very much, you should know that by now.

REX. Yeah but I thought — you could . . . I wanted . . .

LEONARD. No! (*He turns suddenly to the mike, turns on the
record over the monitor speakers, fades it down.*) That was
Miss De Paul. I'm now struggling with another letter on
pink paper — it's from Mrs Joan Parsons saying 'Dear Leonard,
Is it true or false that you were a teacher in another life?'
Well, now, I don't know about another life, Joan, but I was
in this one, yes. I trained as a teacher as it happens, before I
slipped into the record business, and when all that went up in
a puff of smoke, I slipped back into the classroom, until of
course I heard the call of Leicester Sound. I thought that
everybody knew that, Joan. (*Smiles.*) A joke. And a note here
from a theatre group calling itself the Gracious Players,
saying, could I give a free plug to their production of the late
Dame Agatha Christie's *Towards Zero* on Saturday at the
Town Hall, Hinkley, which seats one thousand five hundred
people. No wonder they wanted their free mention. And I'm
now being handed by the ever-dependable Rex, a piece of
paper on which is written 'DON'T FORGET'. And if you
don't know what that means, I do, and I'll tell you in a
moment, for we have a real thriller coming up; but to change
the subject — (*Putting on a record.*) — I have lost some weight.
In fact I've lost so much weight, I'm floating out of my seat,

floating round the studio. They've had to weigh down my trousers with Encyclopaedia Britannicas! (*Normal.*) While our friend Rex is gaining all the time, I'm afraid, he's approaching sixteen stone now, a hunky piece of flesh, can hardly fit into his box. Enough of this gibberish. 'DON'T FORGET' means competition time. We have a stunner for you in a moment . . . till then, let's flash back into the dim distant past of last week. (*He switches on a record; 'It's Gonna Sell A Million'; and turns the sound off after a couple of bars.*) That was better — that was very slightly better.

He gets up, walks.

REX (*entering*). Why do you keep on doing this?

LEONARD. Doing what?

REX. You know . . .

LEONARD. Putting weight on you, you mean — making you an obese lump. It's my rather dismal little joke.

REX. I thought . . . you were the one for the truth over the air.

LEONARD. I allow myself this one slight distortion.

REX. But people will discover, won't they?

LEONARD. No they won't, nobody's ever going to publish a picture of you, are they?

REX. Yes. (*Pause.*) The local press might.

LEONARD (*smiling*). Not with shares in this station they won't. In fact a total wall of silence could be preserved about your real size for evermore. In fact if I wanted I could pump you up steadily to twenty-five stone and then burst you. (*Pause.*) Sorry. (*Smiles.*) Don't worry, I do it to everyone that works for me.

REX. So I've heard.

LEONARD. So there's no need to look injured. You're not, yet.

REX *moves to go.*

REX (*slight smile*). By the way, I've got Capital on the line.

LEONARD (*without looking up*). You'll have to be more convincing than that. Been listening to jabber and gossip, have you?

REX. I suppose so, yes.

LEONARD. Well, don't.

REX (*watching him*). Everybody knows anyway. Are they going to make an offer then?

LEONARD. It's just possible. Everything's possible. I shouldn't bank on it.

REX. For the afternoon show . . . (*Smiles.*) They'll be sending spies up here. They'll be sitting in pubs with transistors and earplugs, listening away. You'll have to give them the whole works.

LEONARD (*looking up*). Will I . . . Get it ready.

REX. It is ready.

LEONARD (*totally matter-of-fact*). You can have a moment longer than usual, because I'm in a generous mood.

REX. Thanks . . . I —

LEONARD (*cutting him off, swinging round to the mike and switching on the monitor speakers, fading down the end of the record*). And now, a special competition. You heard me — a mind-tingling competition. And by my side is the ever-dependable Rex, sweating slightly, what have we got as a prize, Rex?

REX (*nervous, standing by the mike and speaking into it, putting on an almost BBC voice*). We have *their* latest LP — the Yellow Jack's latest!

LEONARD (*brash voice*). Tell us the title, Rex — *please* tell us the title.

REX. 'High Up There'.

LEONARD. That's a fine title — is it a fine record?

REX. It's very exciting Leonard, it really is . . .

LEONARD (*to the listeners*). And you can have it a whole two or three weeks before it's in the shops, one of the very first in the whole country to have it. And what is Rex going to make us do? . . . Well, I think he's been fiddling with his tapes.

REX. I have indeed —

LEONARD. Very posh today aren't we, Rex?

REX. Are we, Leonard?

LEONARD. And what have you done with your tapes?

REX. I've slowed them down — rather a lot.

LEONARD. Slowed them down — we're getting even more posh.

REX. Yes.

LEONARD (*loud*). Tell me Rex, what effect does this have on the listener?

REX. What?

LEONARD (*very fast*). What effect does this have on the *listener?*

REX. What . . . well it . . . (REX *dries completely, stands helpless.*) I . . .

LEONARD *presses the button: a tape of the Leicester Sound jingle cuts off* REX's *floundering.*

LEONARD. Enough of this gibberish. (*Normal voice.*) OK, sweets — this is it. Rex is going to play one of the songs in the Top *Eleven*, and it has been slo-o-o-o-owed do-o-o-o-own, so it sounds a little different. And you're going to give us the singer and the song aren't you . . . Double five three zero four is the number to ring . . . that's right. (*Bogart voice.*) Play it again, Rex.

REX *back in his box, switches on a tape of 'The Proud One' by the Osmonds at 16 rpm.*

LEONARD (*after a few bars, reducing the volume on the monitor speakers, he talks into the intercom to* REX; *off the air*). Sounds a little more exciting like this doesn't it. I shall always play it like this in future. (*Suddenly loud.*) All records will be played at *eight* rpm, and we'll talk that slowly too.

REX *has come out of the box.*

REX. I'm . . . sorry about messing things up, I didn't mean to . . .

LEONARD. Of course you didn't —

REX. You took me by surprise, I didn't think . . . I'm sorry, I won't do it again.

LEONARD. No of course you won't. You won't get another chance to. Now get back into your box where you belong. (*He returns to the mike; switches it to go live again. Loud.*) Rex — what have you done to my favourite song? How's that for first-degree murder — a fine song slo-o-o-owly tortured to death. OK, sweets, who can be the first caller — race to your phones, dial furiously . . . I'm touching the first prize now — all fourteen tracks of it . . . we're handling the two of them

with rubber gloves up here — and forceps, and we're keeping
them in an incubator at night, in case we can hatch a
third. Seriously now — (*He's put his headphones on.*) — we
have a caller; and the first caller is . . .

A GIRL'S VOICE (*on the telephone, amplified through the
monitors*). Hello? Hello . . .

LEONARD (*softly*). Hello there . . . what's your name, love?

GIRL. Angela . . .

LEONARD. Lovely. Have we ever talked before?

ANGELA. No, never —

LEONARD. Fine. You at home Angela?

ANGELA. Yeah — I'm at home.

LEONARD. Good — well, let's go straight into it Angela, into
the unknown . . . (*Signalling to Rex, who switches on the
slowed-down tape again, in the background.*) Who do you
think the noise is, this *slo-o-ow* noise?

ANGELA. Is it — 'The Proud One' by the Osmonds?

LEONARD. Did you say —

ANGELA (*about to correct herself*). I . . .

LEONARD. Angela, you're r-r-r-o-o-o-o-ight! Well done! (REX
speeds up the record to the right speed, it plays a few bars.
LEONARD *signals to* REX *and the volume is reduced.*) There
we go — clever girl. I'm dropping your prize into Rex's
hand, to be wiped spotless, and posted, jet-propelled towards
you Angela. Bye, love. Let's have the next one Rex. (*A
slowed-down version of 'I Can't Give You Anything (But
My Love)' by the Stylistics.* LEONARD *gets up again.*) This
is an easy kill for them — they use their record-players so
much at home, they all run slowly anyway . . . those who
have record-players.

REX (*staring at* LEONARD). I really like it, you know — (*Slight
smile.*) — if I'm allowed to say so, how you always touch
something when you're talking about it, even if it's the wrong
record, like just now.

LEONARD. Yes. I like that too. It's the actor in me. It's what
makes it reasonably good. (*Staring round the studio.*) Where is
the nauseating object anyway? (*Sees the Yellow Jacks LP,
picks it up.*) Have you read the back, with Ross — (*American*

voice.) — the lead singer speaking *his mind.* (*Normal voice.*) Take an example at random — and this is a nice lad from Bolton speaking — 'Ross numbers among his favourite things: walnut ice-cream, honeysuckle, genuine people, starfish, and sunburnt bare feet.' (*Loud.*) You realise we're going to have to play the utterances of this jellied imbecile all this week — the promoters have sent us a long tape, in a silk case, and the station's excited too, they want it to be a lively few days; I keep getting little illiterate messages from Johnson pushed under the door saying, 'Please remember, *maximum* required'. (*He switches on the mike suddenly.*) Hello — what's your name please?

GIRL'S VOICE. Rita.

LEONARD (*slight smile*). Lovely Rita, Meter Maid?

RITA. What?

LEONARD. A reference to years gone by, don't let it worry you, Rita. Have we talked before?

RITA. No.

LEONARD. You listen often —

RITA. Yes . . . yes I do.

LEONARD (*smiles, soft*). Good, that's how it should be. Let's go straight into it then love, into the nitty gritty — who do you think it is?

RITA. I think it's — (*She gives the wrong title.*)

LEONARD. Well, Rita, you're wrong, I'm afraid.

RITA. No I'm not . . . am I?

LEONARD. I'm afraid so.

RITA. You sure? . . . (*Louder.*) I was certain. You —

LEONARD (*cutting her off*). I'm sorry love, you're wrong; keep listening though, for a very important reason . . . bye for now. (*Hughie Green voice.*) And let's go straight in to the next contestant! Coming up to Big John with the news at three o'clock. One down, one LP to go — round, crisp and shiny. What's your name please?

NICOLA'S VOICE (*extremely flat, unemotional*). Hello.

LEONARD. A little louder please — what's your name?

NICOLA (*very quiet*). Nicola Davies.

LEONARD. A little louder.

NICOLA (*loud*). Nicola Davies.

LEONARD. Nicola Davies. That's very formal. Are you at home, Nicola Davies?

NICOLA. Yes.

LEONARD (*suddenly interested*). And what are you wearing, Nicola?

NICOLA. Trousers . . . .

LEONARD. A little louder — you've got a very nice voice, Nicola. You're wearing trousers, and anything else?

NICOLA. Yes . . . shoes.

LEONARD. Shoes, that's an interesting picture, she's wearing just trousers and shoes. Only wish we had television phones, sexy Nicola . . . so, to win this LP, that Rex is just slipping into its beautiful see-through tight-fitting sleeve — who is it, Nicola?

NICOLA. It's the Stylistics and — (*She gives the wrong title.*)

LEONARD. I'm afraid, Nicola . . .

NICOLA (*correcting herself*). No, it's 'I Can't Give You Anything (But My Love)'.

LEONARD. Well Nicola — I'm afraid your first answer is the only one I can accept . . .

NICOLA. Oh . . .

LEONARD. But you were very close — and so, as you've given us *all* your name, Nicola Davies — I'm going, actually, to give it to you.

NICOLA. Oh good — thank you.

LEONARD. Just for you, Nicola Davies, but on one condition — and that is —

NICOLA (*nervous*). What is that?

LEONARD. You listen for just one more moment, because I have something rather extraordinary to announce to everyone . . . I'm going to be running many competitions this week for all ages — but one of them is different — for, to tie in with the great Yellow Jacks' concert here in this city on Saturday

we're running THE COMPETITION OF THE CENTURY . . .
and the prize is actually meeting one of the boys. How do
you like that, Nicola Davies?

NICOLA. Yes . . . what do you do?

LEONARD. And not only that — the winner will ride to London,
after the concert, in *their* car, sitting with *them*, and what is
more they will then spend four whole days in London, the
capital of this fine country, at the expense of Leicester
Sound. That's OK, isn't it? — Nicola?

NICOLA. Yes . . . what do —

LEONARD (*cutting her off*). So everybody tune in tomorrow,
for the first stage — you too Nicola — (*His voice quieter,
smiles.*) — you never know — what your luck might be — we
might even speak again. (*He puts down the phone. Drops his
biro onto the desk. Pause. Quiet.*)

We're off.

Blackout.

Scene Two

In the blackout: a radio commercial.

SHARP TRANSATLANTIC VOICE. We are going DOWN!
DOWN! DOWN! Yes, everything's down at Liptons. Shop at
Liptons where eggs are down — (*Echo effect.*) — DOWN!
DOWN! Bacon is down and what's not down's not up.

SONG. LIPTONS MAKES THE GOING EASY, LIPTONS
MAKES THE GOING GREAT!

*As the song continues, there is a sudden explosion of white
light.
Supermarket. The music of the commercial breaks into pop
music, playing in the background.
NICOLA standing by the fridge, staring ahead, pale face.*

SUSAN's VOICE (*off-stage*). Nicola?

*NICOLA doesn't react. SUSAN enters, stands at a distance from
NICOLA.*

SUSAN. Nicola? Here . . .

*NICOLA glances up. Suddenly SUSAN crosses over to the
fridge, very sharply.*

NICOLA (*surprised, nervous*). What you doing over here?

SUSAN. What do you think?

NICOLA. You shouldn't have come over. You know you're meant to stick to your own counter.

SUSAN. Why should I? I hate standing over there, by myself all the time. I've got to talk to somebody, haven't I — even you! Anyway, I start thinking funny thoughts, after a bit. (*She glances up at the strip-lighting.*) If you stare at those lights long enough, it does that.

NICOLA (*sharp*). You'll be seen any moment, you know.

SUSAN. I won't. (*She feels her tunic.*) Christ, I'm tired after that rush, and it'll soon be starting again. (*Pulling at her tunic.*) I get so hot in this all over. What's that — let's see that . . .

NICOLA. Nothing.

SUSAN (*making a grab for it*). What you got a postcard for, with nothing on it.

NICOLA. Stop it! You'll get it wet. (*She puts the postcard back.*) Look, if I'm seen talking to you, by the camera — (*They both glance up.*) — we'll both get it, won't we? You just have to make a wrong move, and he'll see you, won't he?

SUSAN. Don't worry, I'm watching out. (*She smiles.*) It's coming now. (SUSAN *ducks.*) You know what happened yesterday? Something exciting. What do you think — a cat got in here, it did. Just after you'd gone. Came through the stacks of Ryvita up there, suddenly there it was. *In here!* You know, spitting and everything. I thought it was a Giant Rat, we all suddenly stopped what we were doing and rushed after it, shouting and screaming our heads off. It really got everybody going. You should have seen us. Made a change. Didn't last long — you missed it!

NICOLA. Yes.

SUSAN (*loud*). I wonder if anything else will get in here soon.

LEONARD BRAZIL'S VOICE (*suddenly piping up*). That was — (*Title of record.*) Don't fear, Leonard Brazil is here. Hello there, wherever you are, whatever you're doing, and a special hello to you. (*As if to all the girls, but strangely personal.*) Yes, you down there, I'm saying hello to *you*.

NICOLA. He's quite loud today.

SUSAN. Yes, he is.

L.B.'s VOICE (*running on*). I've got a lot of goodies coming up, and no bad 'uns. Every sound is freshly picked up here, specially for you, that's why they're so ripe and full of flavour. Juicy! You don't believe me, well, it's true.

The music begins.

SUSAN. He's talking a lot today, isn't he?

L.B.'s VOICE. Very soon that special something I promised, Stage One . . .

NICOLA. Yes.

L.B.'s VOICE. Until then, let's move onto the year 2000 and maybe we'll be listening to this. (*He plays 'Long Haired Lover From Liverpool.'*)

SUSAN (*looking into the fridge*). I'm so hungry, aren't you, can't stop feeling hungry.

NICOLA. Careful, what you doing. He'll kill us if he sees.

SUSAN (*her hand inside the fridge*). It's horrible inside here. We could fuse this fridge, you know — just have to get the right thing. (*She pulls at something inside the fridge.*) Once saw it happen, all the food melts slowly, goes soggy and bad, and it all floats in a big kind of mush, you can pour the whole lot out like a lot of soup. (*She pushes the fridge.*) It moves too, you see!

NICOLA. Don't, please . . . I don't want trouble today, Susan . . .

SUSAN (*pushing the fridge*). It moves easily, we could push it down there if we wanted.

NICOLA (*shouts*). Mind! (SUSAN *springs back as the camera pauses. Nervous.*) He's seen us now. Think. You're going to get us sacked at any moment now.

SUSAN. I wouldn't mind that — I wouldn't. Anyway, he's asleep most of the time, the guy who watches it. Up in the office.

NICOLA. No, he's not! When there aren't many customers, like now, he's watching us all the time.

SUSAN. Yeah, he enjoys doing that. It's his sort of game. Come on — (*She calls to the camera, then ducks.*)

NICOLA. Have you see him yet. Do you know what he looks like?

SUSAN. Yes, I saw him through the door once. He's very fat.
I've heard all about him, he sits there all day, with one of his
socks off, picking his toes, and eating the stuff, while he watches.

NICOLA. He doesn't do that, does he?

SUSAN. Yes — he used to be a policeman, you know. And when
he sees a customer taking something, or one of us, he has them
up there, and he says 'He'll let them go'. If he can do what
he likes with them for half an hour, puts his hand down you
know and that — (*She pushes her hand inside twice.*)

NICOLA. You're making all this up, like always.

SUSAN. I'm not. It's true! And that's why you stare so much at
the camera, isn't it? Because you wanted to get noticed —
be invited up there. You want that to happen, don't you?

NICOLA. I don't. Well, it might be interesting. But I don't just
wonder about him!

SUSAN. Maybe he's staring at us, right at this moment,
smacking his lips — about to jump. (*She looks into the fridge.*)
Have you taken anything yet, then?

NICOLA. No.

SUSAN. Have you stopped taking things, then?

NICOLA. No, but they've started searching us, haven't they?

SUSAN. Yes. My mum doesn't believe they search us. She can't
think why they should have to, except for bombs, in case we
had bombs! (*She puts her hand into the fridge.*)

NICOLA. It's coming round again. Careful!

SUSAN. Nicola . . . let's take something now, right now.

NICOLA (*astonished*). What?

SUSAN. Come on — take that! (*She throws* NICOLA *some
food.*) And that . . . and that . . . (*Throwing a huge bundle of
food at* NICOLA.)

NICOLA. Look, stop it, Susan. Stop it, it's coming . . .

*A large can drops out of her hands and rolls along the floor.
At the same moment, the music cuts off.
Silence.*

NICOLA *turns, frightened and bewildered, and rushes out
in front of the fridge to pick up the can.*

ROSS's VOICE. Don't move, folks, stay right where you are, because yes, it's me. See you Saturday.

L.B.'s VOICE. Those few words were spoken by you know who, Ross. I'll be playing some more of his dulcet tones tomorrow.

NICOLA. Shhh! I want to really listen now.

L.B.'s VOICE (*strangely gentle, as if half-aimed at her*). So have you got a lead pencil ready — is it in your hand — are you gripping it — hold it — tight — won't you — because we've come to that moment you've been waiting for since yesterday . . .

SUSAN (*loud*). You're not going in for that competition, are you, you can't . . .

NICOLA. Sssh! Be quiet.

L.B.'s VOICE. Come on, now then, are you ready, because I'm only going to say it *once*, so pin back those ears of yours, and listen . . . ready . . .

Sudden silence.

NICOLA (*loud*). What's that . . .

Just silence.

They've switched it off.

SUSAN (*smiles, teasing*). Yes — they must have known what you were going to do.

NICOLA. They would switch it off then!

FAT MAN'S VOICE (*silky, nauseating, menacing*). Can Miss Lyle come into the office please . . . Could Miss Lyle come here immediately, please . . . immediately . . .

SUSAN (*loud, defiant*). It's not us . . . it's that old bag, seen her nicking . . .

NICOLA (*moving backwards and forwards*). They were only going to say it once, weren't they? How can I find it out?

SUSAN. You can't go in for *that* competition. You won the record yesterday. They wouldn't even let you start.

NICOLA. I must find it out, probably won't be something like this for ages — where's the building that it comes from.

SUSAN. No idea. They'd never let you in, either.

NICOLA. No. (*She turns.*) I'll phone them up then. I know the number.

SUSAN (*smiling*). Can't use that phone. Only for supervisors.

NICOLA. I don't care. (*She moves.*)

SUSAN (*loud*). Mind! Nicola! (*The camera stops . . . the camera pauses . . .*) You'll never get over there without being seen. He's watching now. (NICOLA *stares across at the phone.*)

FAT MAN's VOICE. Miss Lyle . . .

NICOLA. It's worth a try. I'm going to. (*She moves in front of the fridge, sideways, crouches, dashes furiously for the phone; one second pause, then she immediately starts dialling furiously, bending to keep her head down.*)

SUSAN (*calling across to her*). Keep down . . . down. You haven't got long now. Hurry!

We hear a very loud 'engaged' tone. NICOLA *slams the phone down and immediately starts dialling again.*

SUSAN. Probably hundreds of people trying — everybody. You won't get to speak to *him* again.

NICOLA. Sssh!

The very loud 'engaged' tone. NICOLA *slams down the receiver. Immediately she starts dialling again.*

SUSAN. It's coming round, Nicola. (NICOLA *is dialling furiously.*) You're going to get seen! (NICOLA *glances up, freezes as the camera passes.*) it's on you!

NICOLA (*staring up*). Go away . . . (*She finishes dialling: very very loud 'engaged' pips.*) I hate that noise. (*She moves back to the fridge, not caring if she's seen or not.*)

SUSAN. There you are. I told you.

L.B.'s VOICE (*suddenly piping up*). What about that, then? What did you think of that. *Super, dooper* as they say in Russia. That was only the start, remember, wasn't it?

NICOLA. It would happen, wouldn't it?

L.B.'s VOICE. Of course I've been asked to repeat it, say it again for *you* that weren't listening, yes — I mean you. Which is against the rules, and I'll probably be fined an enormous sum of money and get banned for life, but I'm going to, just for you.

NICOLA. Hear that?

L.B. OK, sweet-s. Here's Stage One again. The First Great Stage, and it is: if you could go anywhere in the world you can think of, with one of the Yellow Jacks, which one would you choose, where would you go, and why. (*Jokey voice.*) You're not allowed to choose me, and the *thirty* best ones get through to Stage Two. That's not so difficult is it, in fact it's the easiest I could make it for you — isn't it? And now . . . (*Music starts. He cues the record.*)

SUSAN. Now you know, don't you?

NICOLA. Yes, leave me alone now.

SUSAN. Your postcard's filthy, you know.

NICOLA. Yes, but I can still write on it, can't I?

L.B.'s VOICE. Are you OK then? It's over to you. (*The music coming up loud.*) I'm waiting for you, aren't I? (*Music loud.*) *Blackout.*

Scene Three

The studio. LEONARD BRAZIL *is standing by his desk. A record is playing silently.*
A spool of tape is going round — and we hear LEONARD's *personal jingle over the speakers.*

JINGLE. LB . . . LB . . . LB . . . LB . . .LB . . . (*He turns the volume up.*) LB . . . LB . . .

Behind him, MICK YOUNG, *17 years old, nervous manner, is dragging in four large sackfuls bulging with postcards.*

LEONARD (*flicks off the jingle, swings round*). What are you doing with those?

MICK (*nervous*). I . . . I'm carrying them in here . . .Mr Brazil.

LEONARD. Nothing is allowed in here, you know that.

MICK. Yes . . . Mr Brazil.

LEONARD (*staring*). What are they?

MICK (*very nervous*). They're bags . . . I . . .

LEONARD. Yes?

MICK. Replies from the listeners. Rex is finishing sorting them . . . you see . . . and there're so many we thought you'd like to see them.

LEONARD (*casually*). Did you. (*He puts his hand into one of the bags, pulls out postcards.*) All these are replies, are they?

MICK. You really got them to write in all right, didn't you . . . Mr Brazil.

LEONARD (*slight smile*). I had a ridiculous dream about these girls last night, do you know that?

MICK (*nervously*). No . . .Mr Brazil.

LEONARD (*lightly*). I was in a small park. There was a whole line of them coming towards me — about twenty of them, and they said they wanted to give me a present — a new pair of trousers, but could they first have my old ones to burn. They must have my old ones to burn immediately. (*He looks at* MICK.)

MICK (*bewildered*). Yes?

LEONARD (*turns, sharply, businesslike*). Come on, take these all out again — the whole lot at once.

MICK (*struggling to pick them up*). Yes, of course.

LEONARD. This place is meant to be the nerve centre of the city, isn't it. And you fill it with all this clobber. Go on, we have very little time.

He brings up the record volume and goes on the air. As he does so, REX *enters, stops* MICK *picking up the bags, and they both stand and watch* LEONARD *from the side. At the end of* LEONARD's *piece over the air* MICK *leaves silently.*

That was Peters and Lee and 'Welcome Home'. And now I've got something to say, folks. (*Gentle tone.*) To all of you, I have a message from our little friends, the Po-Leese. They say a lot of people in this fine city of ours have been taking what doesn't belong to them. In plain full frontal language, *stealing* and our little friends in blue have had to go into schools and shops, and put down the deadly purple dye . . . so they can catch them purple-handed. So seriously now, I know times are hard, but keep out of trouble — you will, won't you? (*Tone changes.*) Very soon on this Wonderful Wednesday we have Big John with all the News In The World — till then, let's explode with a raving cataclysmic ditty from 1968, the Rolling Stones and 'Street Fighting Man'.

Explosion of sound. LEONARD *listens for a moment, sees* REX *and cuts it out suddenly.*

What you doing?

REX (*standing staring*). I was watching you.

LEONARD. That's not permitted, especially the amount you do. Your ogling is getting on my nerves. Why do you do it?

REX. Because it really interests me, doesn't it. (*Smiles.*) Have you heard anything from Capital? (*Fast.*) Do you think they're listening now and going to . . .

LEONARD (*sharp.*) That, Rex, is a forbidden subject, and you know it is. Come on, we have three minutes to go.

REX (*still standing there*). Yes, Leonard . . . I wondered if . . . I just happen to have an item here I thought you might like or perhaps even . . .

LEONARD. You could have a quick spot and read it yourself? That's what you were going to say, wasn't it? You're pushing, aren't you lad. I do believe you're beginning to *push*. I've never ever seen somebody begin so early.

REX. I'm not . . . I. (*Quick.*) I'll just read it, shall I? (*He takes out a black notebook.*)

LEONARD. That's the little notebook with all of Rex in it, that you keep hidden in your box.

REX. It's an absurd news item. (*He reads.*) 'And we've just heard that in a Walls factory in Luton, a severed leg was found in a vat of raspberry ripple ice cream. The authorities are checking to see if they've got a cone big enough for it.'

Silence.

LEONARD. Even from somebody like you, that is quite diabolically dreadful. You're a disgrace to this microphone. (*Suddenly looks him straight in the face.*) You are!

REX (*startled*). What do you mean? What's wrong with it? People like black jokes now — I've some *much* blacker ones, you know. They love them — can't have enough. It's what they really want.

LEONARD (*sudden*). You don't have to tell me what they want, Rex.

REX. No, of course not. (*Genuine admiration, quiet.*) I *know* you know.

LEONARD. That's better.

BIG JOHN *enters; a shiny, red-faced man.*

JOHN. Hello there, everyone. (*Smiles.*) Two minutes to go.

LEONARD. The lad's being pushy.

JOHN. Is he? That's no surprise.

REX (*nervous suddenly*). I'm sorry, I didn't mean . . .

LEONARD. We've got to go on to Stage Two in two minutes, go on . . . get out! (*He switches onto the air without a break, fading down the record.*) Hello sweet-s — stand by. Very soon now you'll have you know what — till then, here's . . .
(*He plays something very cheap and nasty. As soon as he's faded out, he swings round and cuts back like lightning into his talk with* REX, *who has left the studio.*)

LEONARD (*loud*). And you make one mistake, Rex, and you're fired — do you hear that? (*Quieter.*) That boy makes me nervous.

JOHN. I didn't know that was possible.

LEONARD (*flicks round, stares at* JOHN). You look particularly cheerful today, don't you, John?

JOHN. Thank you. I'm in very good form, yes.

LEONARD. As usual, you've probably got a train disaster and a couple of mass murders there — (*Tapping* JOHN's *file.*) — and your cheeks are positively glistening   — Bright and Rosy.

JOHN. Thank you. (*Smiles.*) But I haven't got anything really spectacular now — maybe by tea-time something will come in.

LEONARD (*slight teasing smile*). Good.

JOHN. What's this I've just heard about approaches from the Big Wide World, from the actual Capital Radio. Are they going to . . .

LEONARD. You didn't hear anything of the kind. (*Loud.*) *Nothing* of the kind.

JOHN (*startled*). I'm sorry, I didn't realize . . .

LEONARD. No, you don't, John. You see this. (*He picks it up.*) This piece of paper — that is the *Competition of the Century.* (*He holds it up.*)

JOHN (*looking at it*). Yes, it's a real cash box week, this week, isn't it? One minute, fifteen seconds to go . . .

LEONARD. And you know what . . . (*He pauses.*) I've done something which I've never done before, John. I've picked out an average girl for this competition. Yes, I picked out her voice. I home in on her each time I go on the air, home in on that voice. And I imagine her face. It would be funny if she knew, wouldn't it?

JOHN (*hardly looking up*). Really?

LEONARD. In fact, each time I pass by the window, I half expect to see her — a small dot standing right down there, staring up towards here, her spectacles flashing — if she wears spectacles. (*He glances at* JOHN *who is not listening.*) You're the only one that knows that yet, John.

JOHN. Yes. I've got no tongue-twisters today, luckily. One minute to zero. Peppermint? (*He sucks one himself.*)

LEONARD. If there was an earthquake today, or a full-scale revolution, those girls wouldn't notice, not a chance. (*Abrasive.*) I taught kids that age once, years ago! But they weren't like this. (*He taps* JOHN's *file.*) Got any earthquakes locked in there?

JOHN. No thank goodness. Nothing like that.

LEONARD. Perhaps you should have.

JOHN (*suddenly looks up*). You must be enjoying all this anyway — it's your greatest week ever, isn't it?

LEONARD. Oh, I am. I am.

JOHN. After all, you've always been wonderful at whipping people up, getting them to TUNE IN. You only have to say the word . . .

LEONARD. Yes?

JOHN. Just have to breathe over the air. They're all waiting for you now.

LEONARD (*standing over controls*). That's right, John. Got your little furry mascot ready, have you? Go on, *hold it up!*

JOHN (*holds it so that* LEONARD *can see*). Yes, of course I have. Ten seconds to zero . . .

LEONARD. You dropped it yesterday in mid-sentence. Hold on to it very tightly, John. (*He flicks on the switch, fades out the music.*) That was the cuddly sound of — (*He gives the*

name of the record. His tone changes, becoming personal.)
We're coming to you very soon now, love, so don't fret, don't
worry . . . It's three o'clock and here's Big John with all the
News In The World.

BIG JOHN *starts reading the News, world items of extreme
unrest, mingled with local items. As he reads, LEONARD
crosses to the far end of studio, out of microphone range, and
calls out remarks to him, trying to put him off.*

LEONARD (*smiling*). You know, John, I don't seem to be able
to believe anything you say today . . . I'm talking through the
News, John . . . I think your mascot's going to fall . . . (*He
begins to cross over towards him.*) Perhaps you need a tickle.
(*He crosses to* BIG JOHN *who's reading the News unwaveringly
and begins to tickle him under the chin, and then under the
arms, in the ribs.* JOHN *shifts in his chair, but keeps reading.*
LEONARD *crosses to his desk. Sharply.*) It's got no life in it.

JOHN (*on the air*). And now back to Leonard, and that
Competition of the Century.

LEONARD. Our thanks to Big John for reading the News so
nicely and so firmly. Stand by, love, any moment. (*Music
plays. He fades it down.*)

JOHN. Someboy'll hear you one day, Leonard. Always jealous
of people taking away your microphone, aren't you . . .
even for a moment. Always trying to put them off . . .

LEONARD. Rubbish! Anyway, I never manage to . . . (*Suddenly,
really abusive.*) *Competitions have an effect on me.*

REX (*entering loudly and suddenly with a trolley completely
smothered in objects*). Here you are!

LEONARD (*facing him*). What are those?

REX. They're your bribes.

LEONARD (*sharp*). My what?

REX. Your bribes, Leonard — from the girls.

LEONARD (*completely surprised*). They sent all those? Why?

REX (*scrambling over the trolley*). They're hundreds of them.
Watch — nicked from her dad, probably. A T-shirt with your
initials on it, some cheese, some socks with toes, a whole cake
with *you* on it, a walking stick, and lots of photos of themselves.

LEONARD (*staring at them, quiet*). All for me . . . ? (*He picks up the photos, stares at them.*)

JOHN (*moving over to the huge stack of bribes*). You're doing very well out of this, aren't you? I don't know what you're worrying about. You're in the middle of a glorious week. (*Feeling objects, pouring over them.*) We've never had a response like this. Could live off this for a month. (*Casually.*) I wonder if there's anything there for me. (*He picks up the watch, or the cheese.*) I could do with this. (*He pockets it.*)

LEONARD. John! Go and find some more *News*. Something worth listening to, for once.

BIG JOHN *goes.*

(*Urgent.*) We're very late now. (*He glances down at the photos, then throws them on his desk.*)

REX (*looking at the photos*). What were you looking for?

LEONARD (*sharp*). Nothing. I wasn't looking for anything. (*Slight smile.*) What am I going to make them do next, then?

REX (*astonished*). *I* don't know. (*Excited, smiling.*) It could be so many things . . . It's got to be something they can photograph for Saturday's front page.

LEONARD. Christ! Look at you, grinning all over your face. You're as bad as Johnson and all the rest upstairs — not that they ever are upstairs, given half the chance. They'd have the kids tunnelling under the motorway, or buying eighty 'Leicester Sound' T-shirts each before being allowed to win.

REX. Yes — they will do absolutely anything, those kids. They're desperate just to get into the studio and meet you, and then the Yellow Jacks and everything as well!! The last concert the Yellow Jacks did here, a girl asked Ross, begged him to sign her lip. I saw it, and he did and I wondered if she was going to cut that bit off and keep it in a jam jar, so the signature wouldn't come off.

LEONARD. Stop that — you're not going to talk like that in here — understand! *I don't like it.* (*He switches on music, goes onto the air.*)

REX (*as LEONARD does so*). I'm sorry, Leonard.

LEONARD. Hello, sweet. How are you then? Good. I wish you

could see the sight up here. The studio is brimming with your answers, they're hanging everywhere. Rex is just handing me the postcards — perhaps *your* postcard, enabling you to get through to Stage Two. Hurry, Rex! Had a hard job sorting them, have you, Rex?

REX (*entering into the double act*). Yes, Leonard. We've been simply wading through entries.

LEONARD. Up to your knees, were you?

REX. Up to our stomachs in some places, up to our mouths, Leonard . . .

LEONARD. You nearly drowned our Rex, love. Pity you didn't send a few more. (*He begins to read the cards briskly.*) Diane Williams of 30 Sutton Road says she'd like to go to Scotland with Peter and climb mountains with him because he's afraid of heights. Quite a sadist, aren't you, Diane. Thank you for that. Pam Lawrence of 10 Rosendale Avenue says she'd like to go to London with Ross, because that's what the real prize is. I like that, a real realist, there. Pam will go far, won't she. Linda Perry of 18 Horseley Road says she'd like to go to the moon with Ross, that's a long way to go, Linda. Because he looks so like an astronaut, and Nicola Davies of 35 Poole's Road — rather a grubby postcard isn't it, Nicola — says she'd like to go to Kenya with Ken, that's a Nicola-type joke, and go on safari because Ken looks so good in a suntan and so I'm sure, would you, Nicola. You're through *all the way* to Stage Two now, love, and a list of all those that have qualified. Get your lead pencil ready . . . (*Music is playing.*)

REX (*nervously*). What happens if we don't think of something, Leonard?

LEONARD. What indeed, Rex. (*Slight smile.*) Disaster.

REX. Perhaps some sort of race . . .

LEONARD. There is of course something staring us in the eyeballs *right at this moment*! Isn't there?

REX (*staring at the desk*). What?

LEONARD. It isn't original. It's been used in America several times. (*He picks up the T-shirt.*)

REX (*excited*). What is it?

LEONARD. And it's rather cheap, not what they're used to.

REX (*louder*). What is it?

LEONARD. They might just enjoy it. *Just.*

REX. What is it, Leonard?

LEONARD (*swings round*). And it is: they have to make a portrait dummy of Ross, or any of the others, *life size.*

REX. What?

LEONARD. A model, effigy. A dummy of one of the Jacks, out of old clothes, like a guy, stuffed full and life size. That's the idea, Rex.

REX. That's . . . that's pretty good, in fact, it's brilliant. (*Loud.*) It is.

LEONARD. It's not at all. It's not even good, but it'll *just* do.

REX (*quiet*). It's great.

LEONARD (*by the controls*). Christ — listen to that.

REX. What?

LEONARD. You can almost hear all their small ears pressed against the radio waiting for it. The Competition of the Century. (*He brings up the theme music really loud.*)

REX. You knew the answer all the time, Leonard, didn't you?

LEONARD. Rex is coming over with all of Stage Two in his hands.

REX. Here it is, Leonard — all of it. (*He hands him nothing.*)

LEONARD. Thank you, Rex. (*His tone suddenly personal, almost gentle.*) OK, *love,* what we want — what I want you to do *love,* is very simple and a little special, for the next stage of our remarkable obstacle race to get to the Yellow Jacks and London Town, where everything is still possible. I want you *love,* to make in the next two days, a model of one of the boys — (*Laughs.*) — one of the great Yellow Jacks, a model of Ross, or Dave, or Ken, or Pete. 'What do you mean, Leonard, make a model, a dummy, how on earth do I do that, Leonard — that's impossible!' Well, *love,* what you do is you get some old clothes, and paper and stuff it up him, right up and copy his face from a picture, and use some wool for his hair, or go to a gentlemen's hairdresser, or even a ladies'. (*Gentle voice.*) 'Please could I borrow your shavings?' No, seriously, *love,* don't spend any money on it, and get it to me at Leicester Sound by five o'clock Friday. Do you

understand now, love? And the two who make the most
wondrous accurate models will become the finalists, and come
up here. That can't be bad. It's not. So do your best, *love*,
and hurry, won't you. Good hunting.

A blast of music, as he brings in a record.

(*Very abrasive.*) I don't like competitions!

Music up again.

Blackout.

Scene Four

NICOLA's *room. Radio playing in the background.* NICOLA
*pulling out a pile of magazines methodically from under the
bed and from the side of the room, and a pile of cans, packets,
etc. that she's taken from the Supermarket.* SUSAN *watching.*

SUSAN. I don't want to stick around. Don't know why I
should.

NICOLA. You said you would. (*She continues to pull stuff out
into the room.*)

SUSAN. What you doing with all of this?

NICOLA. There's not much time.

SUSAN (*suddenly grabbing a poster from the pile*). Hey! you've
got one of these. Who's it of? (*She unfolds an enormous pin-
up poster of a star, holds it up and looks at it.*) Oh, him!
You haven't done it, have you? Don't you know the point?
(*She lays it out on the floor.*) Got it at shop, did you, off the
market . . . They're from America . . . Don't you know what
to do? You have to wet it. (*She lies down on top of it.*)
Wet it with anything you've got and rub it all over. Rub.

NICOLA (*moviing over to her*). Yes. (*She rubs hastily too.*)
We haven't got time, really.

SUSAN. And the top should sort of peel away. (*She is lying on
top of the poster.*) And you see all the hair underneath, and
you see *everything.* (*She rubs, still lying on the poster.*) It's
not really his body, it's somebody else's and they cut his
head off. (*Loud.*) Come on! (*She rubs frantically.*) It's too
old! (*Loud.*) It doesn't work! (*She rubs again. Loud.*) Why
not. I *wanted* it to.

NICOLA. Probably never did work. Come on — I've lost time now. Hurry!

SUSAN (*lying on the poster*). I took one of these to sex education class, she was new then, Miss Booth, thought she'd be interested. She hit me across the face! Right there! Girls shouldn't have such things and all that. Why not? I saw her flushing it down the toilet, she talked like a dalek, anyway. I couldn't hear any of her sex education lessons, the traffic noise right by me. (*Loud.*) I never heard *anything* at school.

LEONARD BRAZIL's VOICE (*on the radio*). That was — (*Name of record.*) How are you doing then? Yes, I mean *you,* whoever you are, wherever you are, you with the sticking out ears. That's right, keep it up, you haven't got long.

NICOLA. Yes. (*She works even faster collecting all the objects together ready for the stuffing.*

SUSAN. He's hurrying you now.

L.B.'s VOICE (*continuing straight on*). Rex's bulky shape is beside me here in the studio as always (*Sudden mock surprise.*) Hey, he's moving away now, don't leave me, Rex, don't leave me. He's going. How can you do this to me, he's left me. I'm alone and afraid Raindrops might start falling on my head — (*Tone changes.*) — and yours too.

Music begins. 'Raindrops Keep Falling On My Head.'

NICOLA. You know, I think he liked me a bit or something when I rang in . . . He spoke to me longer than the others, different.

SUSAN. He only spoke to you different from the others because he was waiting for the News to come up.

NICOLA (*to herself*). Ready now! (*Worried.*) I'm running out of time, come on! (*She suddenly pulls the dummy out from under the bed, all in pieces, the huge torso, the decapitated head, the hands, the feet, the arms, etc.*)

SUSAN. Look at it! You'll never finish that in time.

NICOLA. Got to. Got to fill it up, make it stiff.

SUSAN (*picking up some of the supermarket objects*). What are these?

NICOLA. Things I've taken from the shop, things I've nicked. They're all going inside. No use to me. I'm sending them all in this.

SUSAN (*picking up a pot of paint*). How did you get all this paint?

NICOLA. Saved lunch money.

SUSAN (*startled*). What have you been eating?

NICOLA. Haven't. Don't need to. So I go for days without eating if I have to. And can.

SUSAN. You'll starve to death, you will. (*Suddenly she picks up the head and a foot.*) Is this Ross?

NICOLA. Yes. He's the easiest to do, his face is very simple.

SUSAN (*suddenly loud*). He's very big.

NICOLA. Yes, I made him big. So he'd notice it.

SUSAN. We can do anything we want with him, now all his bits are here. We can stand on his face. (*She stands on it.*) Can't we? Pull his tongue out. (*She picks up the torso.*) Pull his knickers off . . .

NICOLA (*loud*). Don't do that, Susan. You'll tear him — it'll tear.

SUSAN. Yes! (*Firm.*) You're really stupid, do you know that? Even if you get this ready and Leonard just happens to pick it out, which he won't, even then you haven't really started. He can go on forever with you if he likes, *on* and *on* and *on*.

NICOLA (*determined*). I know that . . .

L.B.'s VOICE (*suddenly piping up*). Hello, how are you doing. Yes, I mean *you*, yes you, with the popping eyes and sticking out ears.

They both suddenly stop and stare at the radio.

I hope I'm not interrupting *you*, am I, because a lady wrote to me to say she had the radio on when, lucky lad, she was giving birth to a baby son, Dominic, and the first sound Baby Dominic heard on this earth was yours truly's ugly grating tones pouring out. I'm getting worse and worse, aren't I? Stop polluting British steam radio — Great belches of grey filth pouring out of my mouth, straight at you down there. In a moment I'll be talking to John Robinson, who's just come out of the army and Northern Ireland and all the old troubles, and he's come home to talk to me.

During this speech, SUSAN *has crossed to the wireless and picked it up right at the beginning of* LEONARD'*s speech and turned the volume down. Then she sings loudly above it.*

SUSAN. Hear him. (*She holds the radio up with* LEONARD's *voice pouring out of it.*) That's the nearest you'll get to him . . . this! It is not any nearer than that! (*She puts the radio down next to* NICOLA, *having turned the volume up.*)

L.B.'s VOICE. And now *you, you* down there who have entered the Competition of the Century, time is running out. Here's some music for you. (*Music begins.*)

NICOLA. Yes! Quick. (*She speeds up the stuffing of the dummy with the Supermarket objects.*) You're going to help now.

SUSAN. No, I don't think I want to, now.

NICOLA (*swings round*). You've got to!

Pause.

SUSAN (*loud*). Why?

NICOLA. Because I'm going to get there. Into the building and see him.

SUSAN (*quiet*). You won't . . .

NICOLA. Come on, there's no time at all now. Paint that yellow, quick!

SUSAN. If I have to . . . (*She takes a big brush and splashes huge dollops of yellow paint on the dummy's body.* NICOLA *stuffs the legs.*) Your room's too small, it'll stink of paint for evermore. You won't be able to live in here anymore.

NICOLA. Good. I want that. Hurry . . . paint.

SUSAN (*sploshing bright yellow paint on the torso. Gradually her paint strokes get faster and faster.*) When they played at Coventry, Ken had a blue belt, the others had yellow as usual. I don't like this colour, sort of sick-looking. They ought to change it. You know I had to get back after the concert — it was twelve or after in the night.

NICOLA (*to herself*). Come on . . . (*She stuffs the legs and the head.*)

SUSAN. I didn't think I could get back. It was raining really hard, straight in your eyes. I got onto the road, started hitching — all these huge lorries went past, enormous. Looked much bigger in the dark. And you know, they all had their radios on. Yes! I could hear. It was Leonard Brazil. It was. He was coming from every single lorry. But none of them stopped.

NICOLA (*quiet, determined*). Come on, quick.

SUSAN (*painting fast*). So I *stood straight* in front of one of them and waved, and he *had* to stop, or flatten me, and he stopped all right, and he opened his door, all smiling and everything, and I got in, and you know what, the seat next to him was still warm, it was all covered with chocolate. Somebody had been sitting there just a moment before — *a girl.*

NICOLA (*to herself*). Faster.

SUSAN. I knew he was going to try to kill me then, yes, on the motorway, in the dark, on the side, where nobody could see, you know, get me on my back and jam a stick of lipstick down my throat, and I'd hear Leonard Brazil on the radio, and suddenly it'd stop, and I'd be dead, and they'd find me in pieces like this — (*Indicating the dummy as she paints.*) — in a bundle, in the mud, been assaulted, flies in my eyes, and all that. And pictures of me on the telly, me being lifted up and wrapped in a sheet, you know. (*Lightly.*) But nothing did happen. Nothing at all. (*Pause. She stops painting. Lightly.*) I wanted it to.

NICOLA (*suddenly very loud*). Oh! Look Susan, it's still not nearly full. (*She stares at the legs and then into the torso.*) We've got to fill it up now . . . (*Moving about, agitated.*) Now!

SUSAN. Put this in anyway. (*She crumbles the huge centrefold picture of the pop star. As she does so, they both suddenly look up with a jolt and stare at all the posters and ornaments in the room. The same idea hits them both.*)

NICOLA (*loud*). Yes! Come on. Everything . . .

They suddenly tear down all the posters and ornaments — everything in the room — and throw it into the stomach of Ross. The action begins swiftly and ends furiously. It lasts under a minute.

NICOLA (*as they do it*). Come on down.

SUSAN (*joyful*). Yes. It's coming down. What's that poster? Come on. (*And SUSAN rips it down.*)

NICOLA takes everything off the chest of drawers, all her furry ornaments . . . everything.

NICOLA. He's got to *be* full.

SUSAN (*loud*). Yes.

> SUSAN's *pent-up violence comes out in her attack on the posters, whereas* NICOLA *is more methodical, but also very fast. The music on the radio ends. They strip the room.*

L.B.'s VOICE (*his tone very personal*). Hello there how's it going, then . . . Yes, *you*? You down there. Keeping at it, are you, *love*, that's good. (*He brings up more music or a commercial.*)

NICOLA (*throwing in objects*). Go on . . . in . . . in . . . in . . .

SUSAN. Come on down. (*She pulls the lightshade off and throws it in.*)

> *They are both exhausted. The outburst ends, the torso is full.* NICOLA *lifts it up. They both stare at it.*

NICOLA. It's finished.

> *Blackout.*

Scene Five

The studio. Night. A phone-in programme. The voice of a caller, JIM, *about forty, on the telephone, coming out of the monitor speakers. The receiver of the telephone is off, lying on the desk.* LEONARD BRAZIL *is standing some distance away, at the back of the studio, smiling and listening.*

JIM's VOICE (*heard first in the blackout*). . . . I mean, don't you agree with me Leonard, about these vandals, hooligans, whatever you like to call them, I mean, everywhere I go I actually *see* things being smashed up, I see them doing it, and writing things up. I mean, I saw some young thugs — I don't want to use abusive terms, especially on your programme, Leonard, and I certainly won't do so, but these men — they weren't just boys, they were grown men, and they were standing round this flower bed of red tulips, and they pulled up every single one, they were pulling them out, by the roots, and treading them into the ground . . . the whole lot . . .

LEONARD (*flicks off the switch to cut off the caller in mid-sentence. Silence. He smiles*). Why do they ring me, explain me that, why don't they phone each other . . . ? (*He flicks the switch on again.*)

JIM's VOICE . . . and even more. And apart from that, I don't know if you find this, I mean as an important person, and obviously on the air — but I mean — these filthy phone calls — people ringing me up.

LEONARD (*turns the volume down, speaks to* REX *again through the intercom*). Is he going to start being rude — I think he is. Thank God I only have to do this twice a week — (*He turns the volume up again.*)

JIM's VOICE. . . . you see what I mean, I don't want to mention anything filthy over the air of course — (LEONARD *holds his finger ready to press the cut-off button.*) — and I'm not going to, but I'm always getting wrong phone calls, people talking to me about things I don't know *anything about!* You know the feeling of course, being a famous person Leonard — somebody rang me the other day, started talking about my horse, how he wanted to buy it, get hold of it, I mean I don't have a horse. (*Loud.*) What would I do with a bleeding horse? (*Suddenly very loud.*) What would I do with a fucking horse in this fuck- (LEONARD *cuts him off.*)

LEONARD (*smiling, very calm*). I'd like to say goodnight now, Jim, thanks for that call, it was a Jim-type call. The time is 9.23 on the LB night show on this Competition Friday in Competition Week, so *hold on tight, love.* It's raining up here, raining black buckets just outside, so let's take a dip into the soft inside of Nostalgia Corner, go back to the golden days of 1967 when London was alive and wriggling and bursting at the seams, remember? Or perhaps you don't. And we were listening to this — some of us were —

Music. 'See Emily Play' by the Pink Floyd. The volume is turned down after a few bars. LEONARD *takes off his headphones.*

LEONARD. That's enough. I don't want any more calls — you've already put through too many. (*He gets up.*) I hate that smell of new paint from the corridors.

REX *enters from the box.*

(*Loud.*) And *also* I've decided I'm not going to do my spot tonight.

REX. What do you mean? Why not?

LEONARD. I have reasons. Got to cope with stage three. (*Loud.*) I'm not doing it. That's final!

REX. Some people tune in specially for it. I mean you *must* do it this week of all weeks . . . we've never had so many calls, so many entries . . . if you would . . . it would . . .

LEONARD. I should, should I? No. (*He gets up, starts searching for something.*) I've never liked them . . . has anyone ever shown you this? The secret of phone-ins! Where is it . . . this . . . (*He starts pulling something out of a drawer.*) When we started, a colleague made these . . . (*Loud.*) Come on out!! (*He pulls really hard. A huge mass of tapes, tangled, without their spools, in an enormous ball, comes out of the drawer.*) Tapes. (*He pulls more out.*) Of the phone-ins, hundreds of them — see? (*He holds them up — a vast amount.*) There are a lot more around us, cupboards full, we should tie ourselves up in it, miles and miles of complaints and shouts and whimpers. (*He holds a piece of tape tight.*) And *frustration! (He runs his finger down the tape.*) You half expect to get scalded by them. He edited them, of course, to make them even more comical, more juicy — this disc jockey did.

REX (*smiling*). Great . . . I must listen to them sometime.

LEONARD. The usual Rex response. Take the whole lot — (*He tosses the mass of tapes at him.*) — they can become your bedtime listening, can't they.

REX (*taking armful of tapes*). There —

LEONARD (*pauses. He suddenly stares at* REX). You realise we're almost alone in this building, we're surrounded by empty corridors. You and me. That's a terrifying thought. I usually have my rest from you at this time.

REX. I know. I asked to do extra time specially.

LEONARD. Did you. (*Staring at him.*) You know, you're the most ambitious thing on three legs I've ever seen.

REX. That's not true. I only want to hang on to my job, don't I? I only want to become good at it.

LEONARD. Only that? I don't believe it?

REX. And I enjoy working on your show, of course.

LEONARD. Don't try to tell me that's the only reason for this fantastic obsessional attempt at efficiency.

REX. Yes, of course.

LEONARD (*smiles*). No it's not.

REX (*quiet*). Of course, eventually I want to get on . . . that's natural, isn't it? (*Smiles.*) I want my voice up in lights, eventually.

LEONARD (*quiet*). That's very good, Rex . . . for you.

REX (*unblinking*). It's your expression.

LEONARD (*surprised*). Is it?

REX. I heard it over the air, before I was working here. I *still* listen to you all the time. I even sit and listen to you at home, on my days off, when you're on.

LEONARD (*astonished*). You don't really do that, do you?

REX. Yes. (*Smiles lightly.*) There's nothing you've said that I don't remember, nothing! I've noticed everything that you've used up here. (*Smiles.*) I'm sort of photostating you really — all the time.

LEONARD (*slight smile*). So that's what you're doing. I wish you'd stop it. (*Moving away from him.*) You know what you are, Rex, you're reptilian.

REX. Yes.

LEONARD. Don't you ever let yourself go — go for a night on the town?

REX. No, neither do you. Do you?

LEONARD. You ought to get yourself another job — I mean that — and quick.

REX. Why should I? This is better than anything else I could be doing. I'd be out of work if I was down there. I want to be different, not a crime is it? And after all you're good aren't you? You are. In fact, Leonard, you could actually be the greatest, the best DJ there's ever been. Couldn't you? Yes, I mean singers become famous one day and are gone the next, but DJs go on and on. You will Leonard — I wonder what the people from Capital are thinking. You must have got it.

LEONARD (*loud*). I told you not to. (*He flicks a switch.*) 9.26 on the LB night show in Competition Week. We all had a great time the open air concert last week, didn't we — it was a true festival, a celebration if ever there was one — the greatest. But I've been asked to point out by the little man in blue — we did leave rather a mess, didn't we. It was six feet high in some places, the farmer couldn't find his sheep, or his bullocks — they were totally smothered, and he had a job locating his lady wife, found her under a pile of toilet paper and cigarette ends. Seriously, friends, let's try to be cleaner next time it'll save a lot of hassle. It's black and soaking wet out now, pelting towards us. Next, the results of Stage Three — stand by, *love,* this is it, now, after something from the summer of '67 when those topless young things with shining kneecaps bounced down the hot streets of our glorious London.

Music: 'A Whiter Shade of Pale' by Procol Harum. It continues to play under dialogue, quietly.

Come on. Bring them in. We'd better get this over.

REX. Yes. (*He doesn't move.*) You're playing a lot of oldies tonight.

LEONARD. Yes. (*Abrasive.*) I'm in a sentimental mood, aren't I? You're much too young to remember, of course.

REX (*smiles, looks innocent*). Too young to remember what, Leonard?

LEONARD. What do you think? (*Abrasive*). Remember before the rot set in. I'm not in any way nostalgic about that time.

REX (*smiling, watching him*). Oh no?

LEONARD. No I'm not. I'm certainly not one of those mooning leftovers wallowing backwards all the time.

REX. No. Of course not.

LEONARD. I know exactly what it was like. (*Loud.*) Exactly.

REX. Yes.

LEONARD (*staring straight at him*). But it's undeniable, Rex, that the music we were producing on that label, seven or eight years ago, was *alive.* That is incontestable. It had gut, it was felt, and it kicked, sometimes savagely. (*He smiles, more flip.*) Because, of course, everything seemed possible. (*Pause. He smiles.*) I was even quite militant in a quiet way. (*Smiles.*) We thought things were changing and all that romantic crap.

REX (*smiles*). Of course you did.

LEONARD. Don't stand there with that idiotic grin on your face!

REX (*doesn't move*). No.

LEONARD (*smiles*). You'd better get on with it, hadn't you, before I decide to take revenge.

REX *goes.* LEONARD *talks to him as* REX *prepares offstage.*

You should have been at the open air concert at the weekend.

It was vile. It was a perfect example. (*Smiles, slightly mocking.*) A grey shabby echo of the time when festivals really were celebrations. Everybody was lying about in lifeless heaps, mumbling apologetically, and getting bitten by horseflies. A few of them were even fighting with each other in the mud. You felt you could have turned them over with your foot, and they wouldn't have been able to get up. I saw one girl, a large girl, with a very big face, she wasn't very young, wandering through a patch of long grass. Her face and also her lips were sort of swollen, and completely ashen, almost blue, in fact, as if she was actually physically dead. I almost wanted to go up and touch her; I felt that if you touched that face it would probably flake into nothing. (*Smiles.*) In fact I haven't got that picture out of my mind yet.

LEONARD *puts on another record in the current top ten. The sound of the record explodes through the speakers as the dummies are brought in.*

REX (*enters smiling with twenty-five dummies on a trolley, piled high*). You've got to make the final choice.

LEONARD. I don't believe it. (*Pause.*) I just don't believe it!

REX (*smiling unconcerned*). What's the matter?

LEONARD. You mean they did it — they actually made them?

REX. Yes, of course.

LEONARD. Dressed and everything?

REX. You didn't expect them to give us nude models, did you? Though they would have if you'd told them to.

LEONARD (*picks one up*). We could be in Los Angeles, couldn't we — except it's even worse. Christ, look, they've even painted fingernails on them, bound to be toenails under that. (*He pulls at their shoes, pulls at their hair.*) Probably their own new clothes too — or their little brother's. They must have worked all through the night on these obscenities. They're burrowing like moles to get up here! Why do they do it — tell me, why?

REX. Because you told them to do it.

LEONARD. You could drop anything over the air into that pool and they'd gobble it up. (*He feels one.*) What have they got inside them — feel this — feels as if it's stuffed with cans, and packets of frozen food! And all their magazines — clogged with them! How many of these ghastly objects are there?

REX. Twenty-eight. Two of them by people we'd eliminated at Stage One, but they still went and made them.

LEONARD (*has picked up another*). This is rapidly becoming a madhouse. We're being invaded by all these. Are they all there?

REX. All the best ones. I put some in the canteen — they're propped up in chairs — as a joke when people come in tomorrow

LEONARD. AS a *joke*? (LEONARD *looks at the labels on the dummies, looking for* NICOLA's.)

REX (*innocent smile*). Nothing wrong with that is there? I've put two in the ladies' toilet as well, sitting on the pan. So which two are you going to have — these are the best. Don't mind the paint on some of them, it got into their hair as I was pulling them along the corridor.

LEONARD. What?

REX. Which two are you going to choose . . . ?

LEONARD. These two'll have to do.

REX (*looks at the cards*). Louise Prentiss and Jane Harris. A good choice.

LEONARD. All right, get hold of them quickly, get this dealt with and . . . (*He suddenly looks up.*) Whose is that one?

REX (*looks at the card*). Nicola Davies.

LEONARD. Really — Nicola Davies. I thought so. Well let's have her instead shall we. Scrub that one.

REX. Why — you chose the other one.

LEONARD. Do as you're told.

Pause.

REX. Have you got a thing about her or something?

LEONARD (*looks up*). No! Of course not. (*Pause.*) I picked her voice out, that's all. I've been using it. (*He looks at the dummy.*) They look more and more like home made corpses — take them away.

REX. They'll make pretty good photos in the paper tomorrow, anyway.

LEONARD (*looks up*). I don't like that.

REX (*looks up*). What?

LEONARD. I don't like it do you hear? You ought to have stopped me thinking of it.

REX. *I* should have . . .

LEONARD (*really working himself up*). What do you think you're paid for? I mean this idea was trash. It was unpleasant!, incompetent, lazy — (*He throws the dummy down.*) — it's trash.

REX. Why?

LEONARD. If you can't see that there's no hope for you!

REX (*smiles*). No hope for me is there?

LEONARD. I need somebody that's going to think, *think*, don't I —

REX. Yes, Leonard, I —

LEONARD. Not just a callous, unquestioning, secret police vegetable . . .

REX. It isn't my fault . . .

LEONARD (*carrying on — a real outburst*). You'd be one of the first to come and take us away, wouldn't you. *Wouldn't you.* Come here.

REX. It was your idea Leonard.

LEONARD. You're an abortion really, aren't you — with absolutely no imagination. Nothing! A complete abortion.

REX (*loud*). I didn't think of it, Leonard, did I — it wasn't me —

LEONARD (*cutting him off*). You're a bloody idiot aren't you.

REX. It wasn't me, Leonard — was it.

LEONARD. Get out of here, go on.

REX *doesn't move.*

Go on, get out.

REX *moves out quickly.*

(*Shouting.*) You're fired. Fired! You really are this time. I don't want to see you in this room again. You leave tomorrow. (*Complete silence for a moment. He faces the record desk and fades out the record.*) That was the Loving Spoonful and 'Summer in the City', and *this is* the Competition of the Century. And now we have come to that solemn moment — the finalists — the two people who are going to come all the way up here. Gauleiter Rex has written the two names out in red ink — you all did so well — showed enormous determination — the greatest in England. But the two who got through — the two names on the card are — Jane Harris and Nicola Davies. Jane and Nicola have won through to the Final. (*Fanfare. It fades down.*)

REX (*quiet, matter of fact, over the intercom*). I can only get one of them, Mr Brazil, the other one has gone to bed, she must have been very confident . . . I've got Nicola Davies for you.

LEONARD. Put her through then, Rex. (*He fades out the fanfare.*) Hello there Nicola Davies.

NICOLA's VOICE (*over the monitor, quiet*). Yes, hello.

LEONARD. Hello there Nicola — I don't know if you've been listening to your radio — but I've rung to tell you, in front of the listening thousands, that you have reached the Final, the final round, of Competition of the Century —

Pause.

NICOLA (*flat, unsurprised*). Have I . . . Oh good.

LEONARD (*louder*). Did you ever think you could make it, Nicola?

NICOLA (*matter-of-fact*). No.

LEONARD. Are you tall or short, Nicola?

NICOLA. Not tall, quite short.

LEONARD. That's funny. Rex said you were tall, I said you were short — you've got a short voice. What are you wearing now, love — what is Nicola wearing?

NICOLA. I'm wearing . . . I'm wearing a belt and top and trousers . . . and no shoes.

LEONARD. No shoes. (*Pause.*) I see. Ross'll like that. I'm looking forward to meeting you, Nicola Davies, tremendously. Aren't you?

NICOLA. Yes, I am. I am, Leonard . . . (*Flat.*) . . . very much.

LEONARD. Good . . . that's good. Nicola's going to be coming up here — I'm sure we'll get on. Tomorrow's going to be an extraordinarily good day, isn't it? There'll be some big surprises, I'm sure, and there's a big surprise now — do you usually stay to listen to the LB spot?

NICOLA. Oh, yes.

LEONARD. Well, Nicola, I have news for you. You are in it, you are in the LB spot. For each week, for those of you who have never listened before, and if there are any they'll be hung, drawn, and fined — LB has his spot, when he unleashes a few things. Are you still there, Nicola?

NICOLA. Yes. I'm here.

LEONARD. Well, you're high up, high up in the LB spot — high in the clouds. And the first — the first LB moment is, it's my birthday today, so I'm told, which is a lie because it's at least two years until my next birthday, and our friend Rex — who is definitely getting ideas — has made a cake. A cake out of melted down records. I have in front of me — (*He puts a book in front of him.*) — a pile of records squashed together with a cherry on top, thank you Rex, that's just the type of cake I deserve. (*Loud, runny voice.*) I deserve it — what am I saying? (*American.*) What's gone wrong with him? Seriously, folks I've been thinking about London, for a number of enormous reasons — London, capital of this fine country of ours. And of course it's the prize in the Competition of the Century. (*Fast.*) I was walking along Carnaby Street the other day, Nicola, it shows how old I am, I can pronounce that name correctly, yes I was there — I was Lord Kitchener's Grand-daughter — the street that made the world swing — you should see what it looks like now — it looks like a museum street, it needs its glass case — especially as half of it has been knocked down. The Americans, I hear, are going to ship it off soon across the seas — it'll be our last export, our swinging relics. They're shipping it off to Texas to stand in the desert somewhere, where it'll ooze away under the midday sun. (*Smiles.*) We mustn't get bitter! (*Funny voice.*) Your mouth tastes bitter, Brazil, it's going black round the edges. Remember where you are. You can't let the side down like this, Brazil. It's an important moment. Brazil, what are you doing? (*Quieter.*) What does he think he's doing? No . . . seriously, everybody, London's still an exciting place — the most exciting place. The only place to be. It's still brown and beautiful. Why brown — why not? Mustn't get obsessed by all our yesterdays, they're gone thank goodness, must get obsessed by all our tomorrows. (*Like a machine.*) Hear hear. Hear hear. Hear hear. Don't spit on the animals. I said, don't spit on the animals — where's Nicola Davies — where is she? Still there, Nicola?

NICOLA. Yes, Leonard, I'm still here.

LEONARD (*smiles*). The rain is slashing at the window. I'm afraid,

Nicola, if it gets to me I may melt . . . I'm afraid. Hear that, Nicola?

NICOLA. Yes. I heard.

LEONARD. No need to fear, Nicola is here. I have a note here, what do DJs really do while they're playing records? That's a good question. I hate to tell you. Some read the papers, some play the stock-market, call up their stock-brokers between records — that's true, folks — some call up their lady friends, and some just play with their stylus. (*Smiles.*) And some long to scream obscenities over the air! The mad DJ. And they all use words so sumptuously for your pleasure. Do you ever listen to your words, Brazil? Never, thank goodness, but never mind. Everybody needs us, after all — (*Lightly.*) — we're the new jokers of the pack, we're the new clowns, we tell it how it should be. And we're going to lick the blues. Each week I try to lick the blues — this time with a flysprayer, I have it out, I'm spraying it, I'm spraying them now, they're falling to the ground, curling up black and dead, legs in the air — we've done it. Don't spit on the animals. We're going to make it aren't we, get through to the other side, of course we are — and if you've just seen some horrible things, on the television, bomb blasts, unemployment, politicians, and all that part of our good old England, and you've switched it off to listen to me, sensibly! Then remember, no need to fear, we're going to lick it, so Shout it out! Things can only get better and better — so Shout it out! We have the greatest day of the century tomorrow, so there's something to look forward to, so let's Shout it out! Yes, you, madam, get out of the bath, and *Shout it out!* And you, love, take your hands away from here and Shout it out! Throw that away, lad, and SHOUT IT OUT! Come on Grandad, SHOUT IT OUT! You too, Nicola Davies, SHOUT IT OUT! Let's have some real music. I said SHOUT IT OUT! LOUDER! I can't hear you, don't spit on the animals — this is nineteen hundred and seventy eight, this is Len Brazil — this is Crazy Competition Week — be there tomorrow — and once more SHOUT IT OUT!

Music stops after crescendo. REX *has entered, stares at* LEONARD. *Total silence, long pause.*

Shit. I wasn't going to do that.

He flicks a switch. A record comes on, incredibly loud. The lights fade.

End of Act One.

ACT TWO

In the blackout we hear two girls' voices singing 'I Can Give You Love' — one of the Yellow Jacks' songs (the words and music appear at the end of the play). They sing the whole of the first verse loudly and slightly harshly to a piano accompaniment, woodenly played.

Scene One

NICOLA's *bedroom. Saturday lunchtime.*
NICOLA *sitting on the bed, brushing her hair.* SUSAN *moving round the room, munching some cheese puffs. A packet with one sandwich in it is on the dressing table.*

SUSAN. You ought to eat something.

NICOLA. I don't need to. Not hungry.

SUSAN (*turning away*). You won't do very well if you don't eat. Here.

> *She tosses* NICOLA *some cheese puffs.* NICOLA *doesn't bother to catch them.*

NICOLA. No don't want anything. (*Smiles.*) Good sort of diet, this competition, I lost a lot. See — it's come off. (*She feels her waist.*)

SUSAN. You don't need to lose any. (*Pause.*) You're getting skinny. (*Pause.*) You look a bit pale, you know.

NICOLA. I want to look pale.

SUSAN. They coming for you in a car?

NICOLA. No, I'm going there.

SUSAN (*turning round the room*). They can't even be bothered to fetch you. Not much left in your room, is there. (*Smiles.*) All this has sort of cleaned it out, hasn't it. I mean the competition . . .

NICOLA. Yes, I put most of it in, didn't I. It all came in useful.

SUSAN (*to herself*). Anyway, there's the concert tonight. (*Smiling, looking at her.*) Is that the lipstick I bought with you — it made my lips so sore, and they itched like anything. (*She rubs her lip.*) Still itch all the time, if I think about them.

I want to get some white lipstick. I'm growing old, do you
know that? (*She looks at* NICOLA.) Yes! How do you feel
then . . . about it?

NICOLA. O.K. . . . Fine . . . (*Quiet.*) I'm going to be all right.
I've been preparing for it. Sat here by the record player all
night, listening to records all night, really quietly so *no-one*
could hear me.

SUSAN (*very lightly*). It'd be more exciting, wouldn't it really,
if you were going to be shot if you lost, or something like that.
I mean, then you really would be nervous. If they were going
to put you in the electric chair, tie you up in a black chair,
and press the button, and — (*Smiles.*) — instead they'll just
give you a consolation prize if you lose . . . that's not very
exciting, is it? (*She picks up the packet of cheese puffs.*)
You're very lucky anyway — you could be going to London.
Never been out of this town have you?

NICOLA. Not really, hardly.

SUSAN. And you've already won that LP —

NICOLA. They haven't sent it yet.

SUSAN (*excited*). Going with them to London, Nicola, you
can't do much better than that.

NICOLA. Well I've got into there anyway — into the radio
building. (*Slight smile.*) I'm going there.

SUSAN. If you go with them — You'll have to be careful of the
heavies — they'll still have their heavies with them, they go
everywhere with them . . . when they were playing in Coventry
in March or whenever it was, and I went, you know . . . and
you know what happened, somebody I saw . . .she was
throwing herself down on the carpet the whole time at the
exit, after the concert, and when they picked her up, she just
threw herself down again, and they got angry, the heavies did,
so they kicked her — not that hard — they kicked her, *one*
did, and so anyway, after a bit, she got up, and went and lay
down somewhere else . . . and she made herself sick or
something on the floor, in a pool . . . so this heavy, he wasn't
one of the biggest, but he came over to her . . . and he said
something, I couldn't hear it, and she didn't move, so he got
her by the hair, not very hard, but he got her by the hair and
rubbed her face in it, like that. I saw it. Gave her a quick
rub — (*She demonstrates with the head of a teddy-bear by the*

bed.) — just once — to stop her doing it.

NICOLA. You've told me before. That's not going to happen to me.

SUSAN (*fast*). I didn't tell you . . . didn't tell you this. That same time, by the place, I was walking along, and I saw this policeman, he wasn't very old for a policeman, he can't have been that old, he was standing in a doorway, I saw him, he was all by himself and he was swearing his head off, he was, with his teeth kind of clenched. And he had water in his eyes, he was crying, well I don't know if he was really crying but his face was all screwed up and red, and really vicious looking, and there was stuff coming out of his eyes. Down his face. He wasn't old. I saw him anyway, it's true. I remember it more than anything else.

The phone rings. NICOLA moves out of bedroom area to the phone. She picks it up and answers it.

NICOLA. Yes . . .

REX's VOICE (*on the phone, very soft, we hardly hear it*). Nicola, Nicola Davies?

NICOLA. Yes.

LEONARD's VOICE (*on the phone, very suddenly*). Hello there, Nicola, this is Leonard here, sorry to drop in like this, we're on the air, love — (*Funny voice.*) — in front of the listening thousands, at this moment. I've just been talking to your fine opponent, Jane, and I wanted to know love, are you OK . . . ?

SUSAN (*shouts*). What's he ringing you up again for?

NICOLA. Yes — I'm very well thank you.

LEONARD. Getting a good lunch, are you — what have you had?

NICOLA. For lunch — some water.

LEONARD. Some water — is that all?

NICOLA. Yes. I'm fine thank you.

LEONARD. You must have something else, Nicola, to get really ready for it.

NICOLA. Yes, Leonard.

LEONARD. The reason I've called, love, is so that we both can tell all the people listening that DON'T FORGET, it's the Competition of the Century today.

NICOLA. Yes.

LEONARD. And don't *you* forget that you're having your photograph taken.

NICOLA. No I won't Leonard.

LEONARD (*slight pause*). OK love . . . we'll be seeing each other very soon, so till then, 'bye, love.

NICOLA (*quiet*). Goodbye. (*She puts down the receiver.*)

SUSAN. Can't leave you alone, can he?

NICOLA. No . . . that's good, isn't it. I think he likes me. I'm going to meet him. (*Smiles.*) I am.

SUSAN. Yes, you really are, aren't you, Leonard Brazil. Do your Mum and Dad know about this . . . ?

NICOLA. They've gone out. I told them — don't think they believed me, or they didn't hear properly — *Mum* would have listened to the programme — but they might have got excited — but they don't like me doing that much.

SUSAN (*hardly listening*). You wearing just that . . . ?

NICOLA. Yes.

SUSAN. You should put this on. (*She pulls out another dress.*) You want to look a bit sexy don't you . . . get him excited . . .

NICOLA. This is OK.

SUSAN. He'll probably give you a bit of a squeeze, quick squeeze at your tits.

NICOLA. No he won't — don't be stupid.

SUSAN. You know what to do don't you, tell him you're deaf in one ear.

NICOLA. Why?

SUSAN. So you can ask for every question to be said twice. Also it'll get him on your side, won't it? You got to try everything you can think of to win. And you'll have to be really on the lookout won't you — he'll try to put you through a lot for something as big as that — he's not going to give something like that away easily, is he? — come on, I'll do that. (*She snatches the hairbrush, begins to brush* NICOLA's *hair.*) He'll probably hold up pictures of Ross in the nude, to put you off, you ought to put spikes on your shoes — so you can kick

him under the table — that's what you've got to do — give
'em their money's worth!

NICOLA (*quiet, determined*). I'm going to win, you know.

SUSAN. Yes; well if the other one wins we'll really do her won't
we? We'll finish her. (*She moves away.*)

NICOLA (*sharp*). Why don't you ever keep still?

SUSAN. Because I don't.

NICOLA. You're always doing that. (*Nervous.*) Please . . .

SUSAN. Why shouldn't I? What's the point of keeping still — I've
never kept still *ever* — (*Moving up to* NICOLA.) Come on,
you're going to eat something now. (*She picks up the
sandwich.*) Come on.

   NICOLA *doesn't take it.*

   (*Suddenly very loud.*) Come on, YOU GOT TO EAT! YOU
MUST! Now open your gob. (*She pushes the sandwich into*
NICOLA's *mouth.*) I might come to London with you, you
know — if you ever get there. Which you probably won't.

NICOLA (*chewing*). You going to be listening?

SUSAN (*slight smile*). I expect so. You ought to stay in London,
don't you think . . . if you get there. We both ought to. Yes.
Get out of here! (*She pushes the sandwich into* NICOLA's
mouth.) Come on — eat it all, get it down. Swallow it,
Nicola. (*Loud.*) YOU GOT TO! RIGHT DOWN.

Long pause. NICOLA *swallows.*

Now you're ready.

Blackout.

Scene Two

The studio. BIG JOHN *sitting.* LEONARD BRAZIL *standing.*
MICK *sweeping up the studio.*

LEONARD (*moving about, speaking to* REX, *who isn't there*).
I want these seats adjusted . . . could I please have these seats
adjusted . . . Where is he . . . (*He swings round.*) And if that
phone rings once more I will have it decapitated. (*Slight pause.*)
It's that oily sod Johnson, he —

The phone rings. LEONARD *picks it up fast. We hear a slimy nasal voice speaking fast on the other end. We catch a few words . . .*

VOICE. Leonard . . . a few words again . . . congratulations . . . just want to remind you . . . Studio A . . . security . . .

As he speaks, LEONARD's *replies are brusque.*

LEONARD (*on the phone*). Yes . . . yes . . . yes . . . Quite . . . Yes . . . All right . . . (*Louder.*) OK . . . Fine! (*He slams down the phone.*) Keeps congratulating me on how things are going. That one was to tell me the precise arrangements for Ross's visit to this building — and not to forget to plug the rest of their tour — and remember you're carrying a bumper lot of commercials —

JOHN (*smiling*). It's going very well isn't it. I haven't seen anything like this for a long time. I like this atmosphere tremendously.

LEONARD (*by the coffee machine*). Yes. (*Quiet, looking at the machine.*) Do you think if one kicked this machine it'd start playing music?

JOHN. Is what I hear true?

LEONARD (*taking his coffee from the machine*). What do you hear, John?

JOHN. That you've been made an offer — that you-know-who have made a whopping big offer —

LEONARD (*matter-of-fact*). Yes. (*Pause.*) It appears I have been offered the job —

JOHN (*smiling*). What? You really have. Congratulations! That's wonderful news isn't it! (*Smiles.*) The station must be really pleased — when you've just started making us a profit. (REX *enters.*) Have you heard? He's been made a firm offer!

REX (*smiles*). He hasn't! Have you, Leonard?

LEONARD (*matter-of-fact*). Nice, isn't it?

MICK. Er — can I just say Mr Brazil how pleased I am that . . . I mean can I congratulate you . . . I mean . . . It's really great isn't it — really great, you'll show them in London.

LEONARD. Yes Mick.

MICK. They won't have seen anything like it, you must be feeling great now, I would be.

LEONARD. That's right Mick thank you. (MICK *grins nervously and leaves.*)

JOHN. When do you take up residence — after this holiday?

LEONARD (*smiling*). I'm not sure, John, that I'm going at all.

REX. What?

JOHN. What do you mean, you don't know?

LEONARD (*smiles*). We'll be seeing about that.

JOHN. Well there's a lot of money there, and the size of the audience — you'll be playing to an audience of millions — you've always been good at that.

LEONARD (*smiling at him, his manner dangerously light*). That's right . . . that's very true John . . .

REX *moves around the studio, getting ready.*

(*Fast to* JOHN.) I think we should put some music behind you today — don't you? Behind the News. A french horn perhaps, sounding your approach — so you seem to gallop in here on horseback, and a banjo under you for lighter parts —

JOHN. Don't think we quite need that . . .

LEONARD. You were a good idea of mine, you know, John.

JOHN (*slight smile*). Of course I was.

LEONARD. My stroke of genius — saying we must have live news and not network.

JOHN (*to* REX, *as he tidies*). It's the best thing that's ever happened to me — I'd been cut back, one of the many to be lopped off the paper; I was lucky.

LEONARD (*laughs*). And I've never been able to take the news seriously since. Like most newsreaders, of course, you have no idea what you're saying — when you read it out. Have you?

JOHN. Of course I do.

LEONARD (*loud*). Rubbish. Last week, I wrote items of total schoolboy gibberish — announcing that the Third World War had just broken out and was due to arrive in five minutes and that the entire Royal family had contracted rabies — and I asked the girl downstairs — Carol — to slip them in. You came in here, sat down, and read them straight out without a blink. (*Grins.*) Without any comment. (*American voice.*) You're highly dangerous, John.

JOHN (*startled*). You didn't do that . . . ? When was that? You had me for a moment. (*Smiles to* REX.) He can take in anybody really if he wants to. (*Smiles.*) This man's rather good, you know . . . he's rather good.

REX. Yes, of course. (*He has collected a tray covered in letters and small parcels wrapped in coloured paper.*) Here's two letters for you. (*He drops them in front of* LEONARD.) And all these presents and good luck cards have come in for the two girls. They've been pouring in all the time before they were even chosen. Some are from old age pensioners, shows how wide our audience is, and some are really aggressive and jealous ones from other kids.

LEONARD (*glancing briefly at his own letters*). Make sure they get one letter each — a pleasant one, Rex. And get this place tidy — we're going to have guests.

REX (*not moving*). Look at that, he hardly glances at his letters. His mother could have died for all we know, or his lady friends could have started eating each other — (*To* BIG JOHN.) — a different one each week — and he'd never show anything.

LEONARD (*putting letter away*). Yes.

REX. And have you heard about his flat? It is totally bare, almost, except for hundreds of books.

JOHN. Yes, I know.

REX. And you know he's hardly eaten all week — so I hear. Gone off his food.

JOHN. The nervous strain — with his offer hanging over him. (*Smiles.*) I hope you're going to give us a great show, Leonard — for all the family.

REX. Of course he is.

JOHN. It's a specially cold day, freezing, out there. Wonderful, isn't it? Everybody'll be indoors, you've got them sitting there already. Probably going to get the biggest audiences we've ever had.

LEONARD (*looking up*). Well, Rex is not going on the air today, is he? He's not going near a microphone.

REX. What?

LEONARD (*lightly*). He's having no part of this competition.

REX (*startled*). What do you mean by that? (*Getting excited.*) What on earth . . .

LEONARD. You're not going on the air, that's what I mean. You've been fired.

REX. What? You didn't mean that, did you? But I've been working things out for it . . . What do you mean. (*Working himself up.*) I've worked all week on this competition — I have, haven't I?

LEONARD (*matter-of-fact*). I think you'd better leave us alone, John, the boy's getting excited. Go on, go and find some really juicy news. (*Slight smile.*) Must have something good, mustn't we?

JOHN (*getting up*). And what if there isn't any?

LEONARD. Use your imagination, of course. Write some.

REX (*as soon as* JOHN *has gone*). What do you mean I can't do anything?

LEONARD. You can't . . . I've decided.

REX. But I must, don't you see . . . I . . .

LEONARD (*dryly*). No. It's not good for you, is it?

REX. What do you mean it's not good for me? (*Loud.*) Why have you decided to do this?

LEONARD. I've told you.

REX. I mean when everything's going so well for you. (*Loud.*) Why?

LEONARD. I don't think you should be let loose, Rex. So I've fired you.

REX. You don't really mean that, do you? Do you? (*No reply; he changes tone.*) Look, please, Leonard, *please*. I've prepared something specially. I have. Just for today please. I've been waiting all week for this. (*Loud.*) I am *asking* you, Leonard. I've worked well for you, haven't I? HAVEN'T I?

LEONARD (*smiles*). You're not going on the air, Rex, and that's final. You're going to run things more efficiently than you've ever done before — for the last time. And you're not going to make a single mistake. Go on.

REX (*doesn't move*). No.

LEONARD *looks up.*

I've got to do something.

LEONARD (*looks at him*). Why have you got to?

REX. Because I want to — (*Matter-of-fact.*) Because I'm determined to. (*Pause.*)

LEONARD. You're determined, are you?

REX. Yes, Leonard.

LEONARD (*matter-of-fact*). You worry me, you know, Rex.

REX (*quiet*). Do I?

LEONARD. You can have just one minute. Sixty seconds. I shouldn't let you, of course — you're still fired. You're leaving after the competition.

REX. Thanks. Thank you, Leonard.

LEONARD. I should keep your thanks till afterwards. You've got a job to do, do it. (REX *is moving off.*) You know this equipment is about to expire don't you. When it gets hot, it smells really tired — probably give out today.

REX. It'll last. It doesn't matter what it looks like.

LEONARD. One wouldn't want to do an operation with rusty instruments would one? (*He looks at the equipment.*) This is all really tawdry.

REX *comes back in quickly.*

REX. There's one of them out there.

LEONARD. One of them?

REX. One of the girls.

LEONARD. Well bring her in of course. Don't let her wait out there.

REX *goes out.*

(*Matter-of-fact.*) Better see what we've netted, hadn't we.

REX (*coming back with* NICOLA). Here.

LEONARD. Hello. (*Pause.*). Which one are you?

REX. Nicola.

LEONARD (*gently*). Let her speak for herself.

NICOLA. Nicola Davies.

LEONARD. Nicola Davies. (*Pause.*) I . . . thought you'd look a little different . . .

NICOLA (*embarrassed*). Oh . . . Did you?

LEONARD. Do I look different?

NICOLA. No — not really.

LEONARD. So you're in the studio now. (*To* REX.) Have they checked her downstairs?

REX. I don't think so — she just wandered in — after they'd done the photo outside.

LEONARD. You better do it. (*To* NICOLA, *gently*.) I'm afraid it's ridiculous, but everybody that comes up here has to be submitted, that's what they call it, to a bomb check. I'm sorry . . . it ought to have been done downstairs.

NICOLA. Oh . . . yes. I didn't know.

She opens her bag.

LEONARD. Rex'll do the honours. (*As* REX *searches her.*) We get hoaxes all the time — twice as much at night. Last week somebody phoned in to say there was a purple bomb, whatever that meant. (*To* REX.) That's OK. Thank you. (*He smiles at* NICOLA.) You like to sit down — careful where you sit . . . Do you want something to eat? We'll try to get you anything you like.

REX *crosses over to the box.*

NICOLA. No thank you.

LEONARD. We're nearly ready for you. (*He puts his headphones on;* REX *is in the box.*) OK, *stand by.* Where's the other one? (*He presses a button. There is a roar of music, really loud.* NICOLA *starts.* LEONARD *fades the music down. To* NICOLA.) Don't worry, nothing in the world to worry about. (*The music fades down; the red light goes on. Into mike.*) Stop where you are! Don't switch off! For I, LB, am here.

This is Crazy Competition Week. This is the final programme — how are you all? On this savage cold day . . . it's warm up here, though. So this is the Big One. For me, too. We've all got to it, and we're going straight into it, folks. (*Slight accent.*) Get the bleeder over and wrapped up. Both girls are smiling, just a little bit tense; we'll be meeting them in a moment. Right now, let's hear one of the prizes in full flow — and he'll lead us into a few bubbling commercials —

ROSS's VOICE (*on tape*). The things I don't like — that's a difficult one. I like most things.

LEONARD (*cutting off the tape. Looking at her*). Know that voice?

NICOLA. Yes — it's Ross's voice.

LEONARD. Rex — we're minus one girl. (*He smiles, flicks a switch.*)

ROSS's VOICE. I don't like violence — of any sort, of course, or people that provoke it, create it, you know, exploit it, they're criminals really, aren't they?

LEONARD (*switching it off*). He's in fine form, isn't he?

NICOLA. Yes.

LEONARD (*calm, smiling*). They're waiting for the Competition of the Century down there — (*Looking at NICOLA.*) — and we may not be able to give it to them. (*He flicks the switch on again.*)

ROSS's VOICE. I mean *we* don't use violence — I know people, some morons and journalists, have said so, but every-body just has a party when we play.

LEONARD. Got a good voice, hasn't he?

NICOLA. Yes.

ROSS's VOICE (*in the background as they talk*). And I don't like parasites, journalists, reporters, people that criticise.

LEONARD (*calm, smiling*). Rex — come here.

REX *immediately comes down from the box.*

ROSS's VOICE (*as REX comes down*). And write malicious things about people . . . and also I don't like people that get above themselves.

LEONARD *switches him off.*

LEONARD. I was thinking, we'd better give them something
to drink, something a little strong, so they don't worry.

REX. That's a good idea.

LEONARD. Go and arrange it. (REX *moves.* LEONARD *still
very calm.*) And you'd better find the other one, hadn't you,
wherever she is, we need her in one minute —

REX (*smiles*). Right, Leonard. (*He goes.*)

LEONARD (*to* NICOLA). You OK?

NICOLA (*quiet*). Yes.

LEONARD *flicks the switch again.*

ROSS's VOICE. I'm not a prude — Christ, you've only got to
ask Ken or Dave, or any of my friends, but I really don't like
sex where it doesn't belong, I mean —

LEONARD *switches it off.*

LEONARD (*matter-of-fact*). You better come and sit over here
love . . . please. Plenty of time, there's nothing to worry
about. (NICOLA *moves over to the chair by the microphone.*)
Looking forward to it? (*Pause.*) Are you?

NICOLA. Yes . . . I am.

LEONARD (*as* NICOLA *crosses*). Good. Don't suppose you ever
thought you'd be here.

NICOLA. No — I sort of hoped —

LEONARD. And you are. You're here. (*Quiet.*) This is the big
one, Nicola. You want to listen to him, do you? (*He flicks
on the switch as he settles* NICOLA *into the chair, adjusts its
height, tests its distance from microphone.*) Are you
comfortable?

NICOLA *nods; as this happens,* LEONARD *stares at her,*
ROSS's *voice booms loud from the speakers in background.*

ROSS's VOICE. I mean I agree with that too, and I don't like
women who swear. I like them to be — I know this is corny — I
like them to be feminine, I'm afraid so, and . . . I know this list's
getting kind of long, but you know one thing I really don't
like is dirty cutlery. I mean it happens in England, it's much
better in the States, but you book in to a really good hotel,
and you wake up in the morning for your breakfast, and the
first thing you see is dirty cutlery, really filthy cutlery, I mean

people don't work in this country, I mean that's the trouble really, isn't it, and somebody really has got to do something . . . I like cheerful music.

LEONARD *switches him off as* REX *enters.*

REX. She's here.

JANE *enters.*

And she's been checked.

LEONARD. Hello, I'm Leonard — cut it fine, didn't you?

JANE. I'm sorry. I couldn't find it. I am sorry — it's not easy to find.

LEONARD. It's OK, love, you're here now. We're ready to go. (*To* REX.) Have you got the drink?

REX. Yes I have. (*He produces a bottle, moves to get glasses.*)

LEONARD. Come and sit here — do you want a drink?

JANE. I don't know.

LEONARD (*pours some out*). Come on, have some, it won't bite you.

NICOLA *drinks.*

REX. Jane doesn't want any.

LEONARD (*jocular*). Don't know why we don't give them vitamin injections as well. Nothing to worry about, girls, I'm just going to ask you a few questions, don't worry about anything I might do, I'm not going to sit here, I may roam about . . .

REX (*producing roses from a tray on the side*). I thought they'd like a rose each — a present from Leicester Sound — two white roses, make them look nice —

LEONARD (*lightly*). They look nice anyway — don't you. Do you want to wear them? Rex's little gift.

JANE *nods;* REX *pins a rose on her;* LEONARD *hands a rose to* NICOLA.

(*To* REX, *referring to* JANE.) She needs to be a little higher —

REX. Yes . . . That was a low-key start.

LEONARD. Of course — this is a family show. (*He puts on his headphones.*) OK, that's enough, stop fiddling with her —

(REX *stops fiddling with* JANE *and returns to his box.*
LEONARD *smiles. To* GIRLS.) Now don't worry, nobody's
going to get hurt, are they? (*Flicks switch.*) Before the
commercials that was the one and only Ross, who'll be
entering this building very soon. We have the two lucky and
lovely girls with me — Hello Nicola.

NICOLA. Hello.

LEONARD. And now Jane — who's looking very composed . . .
Rex has just given them a couple of roses — one of course
white, the other is red — we have a real War of the Roses
coming up here. I wish you could smell them, breathe into the
mikes, girls. (JANE *leans forward, he restrains her.*) Here come
the questions, glistening on a silver tray. (*He picks up some
white cards from desk.*) Thank you, Rex.

REX (*loud, excited, important*). We've got one of the biggest
audiences we've ever had — it's a great sight. The studio's
looking very fine. The competitors are in perfect condition,
sleek and healthy, and there's traffic jams for miles —

LEONARD. Enough of this gibber! You're going to make some
noises, aren't you?

REX. I am indeed Leonard — I'm going to make this noise for a
right answer . . . (*Loud bell.*)

LEONARD. That's a nice noise for a right answer.

REX. And this noise for a wrong answer . . . (*Loud vicious
buzzing noise.*)

LEONARD. That's a grisly noise for a wrong answer.

REX. And I'll be making this noise for 'Don't Knows' . . .
(*Funny, irritating noise.*)

LEONARD. Yes, girls — *No* 'Don't knows' — have a guess. If
you say, 'Don't know', — (REX *makes the 'Don't Know'
noise.*) you lose a life; if you lose three lives, you're out of
the game, and if it's a tie —

REX. If it's a tie —

LEONARD (*quiet*). We want *you* to vote, ladies and gentlemen,
for who put up the best show — so keep your ears skinned,
or peeled, or however you like your ears done.

REX. Where are the other questions, Leonard?

LEONARD. In my head, Rex.

REX. And —

LEONARD (*cutting him off suddenly*). And this now — this here — is — The Competition of the Century. (*Quiet, matter-of-fact.*) Jane and Nicola are the contestants; I, Len Brazil, am putting the questions. (*Quiet.*) 5, 4, 3, 2, 1, ZERO! And the very first question is for Jane . . . And the question is: Jane — (*Quick.*) — How old is Ken?

JANE. Ken? He's . . . twenty-one.

Bell rings loudly.

LEONARD. Correct! The lady is correct. Do you know how many months?

NICOLA (*fast*). Six.

LEONARD. It's Jane's question, Nicola.

JANE. Six months.

Bell rings again.

LEONARD. One point to Jane. (*Suddenly loud.*) Jane has one point! (LEONARD's *manner begins to quicken, his DJ instinct coming out despite himself.* LEONARD's *highly charged inner state during the competition should be underlined by his constant movement away from his chair and his total absorption in* NICOLA *to the exclusion of* JANE. *He stares at* NICOLA, *touches her chair, stands over her during her long speech.*) And the first question for Nicola is — the question in Round One for Nicola is, and she's looking very calm . . . is — What is Dave's favourite food — and when does he like to eat it?

NICOLA. Dave's favourite food . . . it's fresh . . . it's home-made bread, and he likes it in the morning — (*Silence, nervous.*) — at sunrise, I think.

Bell rings loudly.

LEONARD (*staring at* NICOLA). That's correct, Nicola. That's the answer that was wanted. You're doing fine, Nicola. So is Jane, both of you are doing fine. (*He has got up, is moving around past his mike.*) Round Two of the Competition of the Century. Another Nicola question . . . Tell me, Nicola, which famous historical and Shakespearean character is traditionally associated with Leicester?

NICOLA. What? (*Pause.*) I . . .

LEONARD. A famous character by Will Shakespeare, associated with this fine city of ours. Have to hurry you —

NICOLA. I'm sorry, . . . I . . . I don't know.

Very loud buzz.

LEONARD. You mustn't say that, Nicola, I'm afraid . . . it's not allowed. So you have to lose a life, don't you. (*'Competition' voice.*) Nicola has lost a life. Do *you* know, Jane?

JANE (*about to reply, then decides not to*). I . . . I . . . (*She shakes her head.*)

LEONARD. Careful . . . NO 'Don't knows'. (*'Competition' voice.*) Neither of the girls know. Which is a surprise! The answer is King Lear — the man with the long beard. (*He moves, picks up the next question. Loud.*) And now Jane, what is the name of the new office block near the prison?

JANE. That . . . it's called . . . I think it's called The New Walk Centre.

Bell rings.

LEONARD. Correct. She has given a right answer. Well up on this fine city of ours, aren't you. Good. (*Funny voice.*) It's completely changed since I was a lad here. It's been torn up and re-planted. You've got two points now, Jane. You're doing well. You're both doing well. Here's another question for you, Nicola Davies — wait for it — when was the Haymarket Centre opened? — Nicola — the great Haymarket Centre. What was the year when its full glory was seen?

NICOLA. I . . . I . . . (*She bites her lip.*) Was it about ten years ago?

Loud 'Wrong answer' noise, repeated twice.

LEONARD. That's the wrong answer, I'm afraid, Nicola. It wasn't ten years ago, no.

NICOLA. Sorry, I — I don't know these sort of questions.

LEONARD. You mustn't say that, Nicola — must have a go, got to have a go at everything — the atmosphere beginning to get a little tense here — not to worry. Nothing to worry about. The year was — (*Loud.*) — 1971. Of course. And our great thanks to Alderman Townshend for setting those questions. There are a lot more I may use later. The score is three points to Jane, and Nicola Davies is trailing behind with one point. Round Three now folks, of the Competition — which is carrying the greatest prize we have ever offered. My questions start here, girls, this is the first one. I'm going to say some words now . . . rather fast. I want you to tell me six of them. Ready Nicola. I'm going to say them very very fast, so be on the look-out. (*He fires the words out sharply.*) Killer, bottle, Junk, Rifle, Tune, Cheeseburger, Sickroom, Commercial, Knife, Disaster, Stereo, Limousine, Tube, Scar, Women's Lib, Cash Quickie, Needle, Platform, Pill, Dungaree, Snow ball, Lump, Oil, Rape, Fire, Neddy, Assassin, Cardboard, Vegetable. (*Pause.*)

NICOLA. Assassin . . . Bottle . . . Needle . . . (*Pause, she begins to panic.*)

LEONARD. That's only three, Nicola . . . Three.

NICOLA (*biting her lip*). Oil . . . Pill . . .

LEONARD. Have to hurry you now . . . Something you ought to know about, being a woman.

NICOLA (*pause*). Women's Lib.

Bell rings loudly.

LEONARD. Well done Nicola — well done. You now have two whole points, yes you do. (*He turns to* JANE.) You thought I was going to do the same to you, Jane, didn't you?

JANE. Yes.

LEONARD. But I'm not! (*Fast.*) Yes I am. Six please of the following. (*Very fast, even louder.*) Chocolate, Wire, Ratings, Tank, Plastic, Movie, Goldfish, Shares, Black, Judge, Union, Red Grass, Steel, Sniper, Index, Trash, Hit, Disco, Chart-climber, Bomb, Cell, Beans, Hook, Barrier, Kite, TV, Kennel, Motorway.

Silence. JANE *stares at him.*

Six please, Jane, quickly —

JANE. Chocolate . . . Motorway. (*Silence. She panics, head in hands.*)

LEONARD. Quick Jane, I have to hurry you, I'm afraid. (*Pause.*) You're running out of time.

JANE (*panicking*). I don't know.

Very loud 'Don't know' piercing noise.

LEONARD. I'm afraid you lose a life too, Jane. (*'Competition' voice.*) Jane loses a life! Both have lost a life now. Neck-and-neck. That's OK, nothing to worry about. Doing very well, Jane. (*He stares at* NICOLA.) Nicola is sitting very still. This is the Competition of the Century. What I want you to do now Jane, is, in your own words, talk about a subject I will give you for *one whole* minute. And the subject is — Jane is smiling, she's straining at the leash — and the subject is . . . folks . . . 'Why do I want to go to London', if indeed you do. It is of course just one of the prizes of this Competition. From now!

Silence.

JANE. I . . . I . . . want to go there . . . to London because I've always . . . (*She stops.*) Are you, are you allowed to repeat things, words?

LEONARD. Yes. You're allowed that. Come on.

JANE. Because, because, I've always wanted to go there . . . and there's a shop in a street, I don't know which street, I saw it . . . this shop, late at night . . . when I was there once, in London, it's the only time I've ever been, and it was open at that time, I mean when shops aren't open, really, and so I wanted to go there, it had big posters in it, very very big posters, some of pop stars, some of politicians, and things, and one of a very fat woman with no clothes on . . . and it had flags all round, the shop did, I mean, and pictures, and names of streets, and souvenirs, cigarettes, and everything. And there was music coming out of it, very loud . . . right out into the street . . . be good to go and shop there. And I mean go and see things, that you know are famous, always been told about, and buy clothes, and look if you can't buy, because there are clothes shops everywhere, not like anywhere else, and see everything, all the night life . . . and I want —

Bell goes.

LEONARD. Well done Jane, thank you for that. That was very well done, wasn't it? Very good Jane, Excellent. I'll give you three out of five for that. So now Jane has six whole points all to herself. 'Six — points — Jane!' And now Nicola Davies, the subject for you is — (*Pause. He stares at her.*)

NICOLA. Yes?

LEONARD. The subject on which you've got to talk for not less
and not more than one minute is — wait for it — (*Loud.*) —
the last pop concert you went to. (*Pause.*)

NICOLA. The last . . . the last pop concert I went to . . . it was
here in Leicester — (*She swallows.*) — and Ross and the group
were playing, and I queued to get in for a long time . . .

LEONARD. How long? How long did you queue for, Nicola?

NICOLA (*completely thrown by his interruption*). I . . .

LEONARD (*staring at her, quieter but matter-of-fact*). How
long did you queue for, love?

NICOLA. I don't know, not . . .

'Don't know' noise, very loud.

LEONARD. No sorry. We don't count that! Rex is a little trigger-
happy, watching out for 'Don't knows'. Come on Nicola.

NICOLA. We queued for a day and a night, I think . . . it was
a bit wet . . . you see, and the stone, the pavement, was very
hard and cold, much harder than you think — because we
slept there you see . . . it was all right and . . . and then a man
came up, it was late you know then, dark and everything,
and he'd come to sell us hot dogs and things, he came out
there and he set up along the side of the queue, it was a very
long queue, and then soon another . . .another came up out of
the dark, and then there was another one, till there were
lots and lots all along the line, really close. (*She looks up.*)

LEONARD (*staring at her, very close*). Go on Nicola! Keep going.
You're doing fine. You've got to keep going.

NICOLA. Oh! I thought it was enough.

LEONARD. I'm afraid it's not.

NICOLA. Oh . . . and . . . (*Lost for words, she is extremely
nervous.*) — and then we went inside . . . and the concert . . .
and it was them of course, and it was, you know . . . well it
was all squashed — and some people rushed up and fought to
get close — and there was a bit of biting, and that sort of
thing, when they called out to us; they seemed a long way off —
a very long way away, in their yellow and everything. They
weren't loud — but they made you feel — I felt something
come up, you know, a little sort of . . . (*A second of slight*

clenched feeling.) I got, you know, a bit worked up inside . . .
they were moving very slowly on stage like they'd been slowed
down, made me feel strange — then they held things up,
waved it at us, smiling and everything, they waved yellow
scarves, Ross had a bit of yellow string he waved, I think it
was, a bit of yellow rope, and I half wanted to kick the girl
in front of me or something because I couldn't see; all the way
through I had to look at her great back, pressed right up against
it. I remember I half wanted to *get at it. Move it.* And I nearly
dropped a ring. (*She pulls at her finger.*) I'd been pulling at,
put it on specially. (*Very nervous, she smiles.*) If you drop
anything it's gone for ever you know — can't bend down if
you're standing — (*Smiles.*) — and if you drop yourself . . .
then you'd be gone. When you rush out at the end, you can
see all the millions of things that have been dropped shining
all over the floor, nobody gets a chance to pick them up.
And then it was finished — you know, the concert, and I came
outside. It was cold, I was feeling a bit funny. Just walked
along out there and I thought maybe I was bleeding. I looked
but I wasn't. Some people like to be after a concert . . . but I
wasn't.

Pause. Bell rings.

LEONARD. Well done Nicola! That was very very nice. Fabulous,
wasn't it, folks, fabulous. I'll give you five whole points for
that. The very most I'm empowered to give. You now have
seven whole points. Now what we want you to do is to sing
a song, one of the Yellow Jacks' songs, and you must try
not to get any of the words wrong. Rex knows the words, and
he'll be watching . . .

NICOLA *gets down off her chair, moves away.*

(*Sharp, still his DJ voice.*) Where are you going, Nicola . . .

NICOLA *half turns.* LEONARD *presses a button; covering
music bursts out, the volume then dips.*

(*Louder.*) Where are you going?

NICOLA (*turns, faces him*). I was . . .

Pause. Music playing.

LEONARD. Where on earth do you think you're going?

NICOLA. I . . . I wanted a glass of water.

LEONARD (*calm*). You don't walk away like that, do you —

you can't leave the room, Nicola — we're in the middle of a competition, don't you realise —

NICOLA. I know.

LEONARD. You've got to stay here, till we finish. (*He stares at her.*) Haven't you . . . (*She doesn't move.*) Haven't you?

NICOLA. Yes, I . . . just wanted for a moment —

LEONARD. Come back here. We're on the air. Rex will get you something afterwards. (*He flicks the switch, the music dies.*) We're here, never fear. Nicola's just had a little accident, went for a walkabout — (*'Competition' voice.*) in the MIDDLE of the Competition of the Century! Extraordinary, but she's back now. The question is, Nicola, Nicola, now sing a song, and the song is 'Yellow Blues'. Stand up Nicola will you; Nicola is standing up, and remember the words must be right.

NICOLA. Yes.

Pause. She is standing, begins to sing, almost finishes a verse,* then very loud 'Wrong Answer' noise.

LEONARD. You've gone wrong, I'm afraid, Nicola. No points. Jane now, it's your turn. Your song is 'I can give you love' by the Yellow Jacks. Like to stand up for it? Jane is standing up now! (*Fast.*) Rex is sweating, we're all sweating, the girls have been chewing our fingers down to the bone. Ready Jane.

JANE *begins to sing*; very quiet. It lasts longer than* NICOLA's; *eventually the 'Wrong answer' buzzer goes.*

Jane, you're wrong this time, I'm afraid. No score for that round at all. But I think I'm going to give her a point, because she lasted quite a long time. Well done Jane. The girls have nice voices, don't they, pity we couldn't hear more of them. And now . . .

JANE. Can I . . . can I change places, I can't really . . . I mean I can't concentrate here . . . because of the lights up there, and him up there. (*She looks upwards at* REX's *box.*)

LEONARD (*fast*). Jane's asked to change places, we'll allow that, but what we'll do is — I'll ask you a question and then you both have to change places, run round the table, and the first one there, will have their microphone switched on, and will be able to try to answer. (*He looks at* NICOLA; *smiles.*) Ready

---

* Words and music at end of play.

to run, girls! And the question is — what were the names of the four Beatles. Ready — steady — GO! (*They rush round the table, the long way. As they do so.*) The girls are running now — running round . . . and it's Jane who's there first, Jane who gets there. Now the Beatles.

JANE (*she struggles*). Paul McCartney, John . . . John . . .

LEONARD. Have to give their surnames too.

JANE. John . . . and Ringo . . . John . . .

LEONARD. Have to hurry you.

JANE. I can't . . . sorry.

LEONARD. You must know the names of the Beatles. (*He smiles.*) Now Nicola Davies, it's your big chance.

NICOLA. John . . . and Ringo . . . I can't remember the other one. (*She looks at him. Deliberate.*) I don't know the other name.

Very loud 'Don't know' noise.

LEONARD. Nicola's lost another life because of that. George Harrison, of course, was the answer. Nicola's only got one more life to her. Nothing to worry about. Now quick round we go again, we'll run before the question. Now! And they're off again, it doesn't take them long, panting and (*Loud.*) — round they go. (JANE *rushes round, but* NICOLA *walks it, not trying at all.* JANE *easily gets there first.*) That was about equal that time, I think — so we'll move on to the next question. (*He looks at* NICOLA.) To the final question of the Competition of the Century. And the great question is . . . (*Pause.*) Wait for it, who can do the loudest scream for Ross and the boys? Who can do the very loudest scream? Right now, watch the windows, Rex! And you at home, watch your radio, because they may break your sets, in fact they probably *will break* them. And shatter all your ornaments. Nicola Davies is first. You do a scream for us now, Nicola. (*Silence.*) Come on Nicola, do a scream. That's all you have to do. (*Funny voice.*) I'm sure she can do it. (NICOLA *sits still. Silence.*)

Come on Nicola. (*'Competition' voice.*) You can do that, can't you, used to doing that. (NICOLA *looks up, opens her mouth slightly, swallows hard; no noise.*) You can scream for the boys, can't you. A really loud one. That's why you're here isn't it? (*Louder.*) Isn't it! You haven't got long, Nicola. (NICOLA *looks up, lets out a half-hearted scream.*) There!

She's done it! That wasn't a very loud one, was it, but now let's see what Jane can do. Ready Jane, just a scream for them.

JANE *sits up straight, lets out a very long scream — which starts loud, gets louder and louder and very very long.*

Jane wins that. Jane wins that point. That is the end of the Competition of the Century, and what is THE SCORE?

REX (*calls*). Very close, Leonard, very close indeed.

LEONARD. The scores are very close, so we are in fact going to invite you to cast your votes for the winner of our prize, going off with the Boys, to the centre of the universe, London Town. So ring us, on 55304, 55304, as quick as *you* can, as from NOW. Just say 'Jane' or 'Nicola', that's all we require, if it's engaged, just dial again at once. And hurry, we're waiting, high up here, in our little box; put us out of our misery.

REX (*shouts*). He's here. Ross has arrived!

LEONARD. And we've just heard, Ross is here, in the building, we've just felt the tremor go through it, and so, while we wait, butterflies swarming in our stomachs, let's have some proper music, a snatch of Rossini's 'Thieving Magpie', followed by a razor-sharp commercial or two. (*He puts on the music. They sit as it plays loudly. A long pause. Total stillness. To the GIRLS.*) You can get down now girls, if you want. (*He calls.*) Rex — get the girls a cup of tea. (*He looks at them.*) Do you want a cup of tea?

JANE *nods.* MICK *enters, grinning happily.*

NICOLA (*quiet*). No thanks.

LEONARD (*his manner suddenly very quiet, withdrawn; to REX*). Get Jane a cup of tea. And Nicola a glass of milk. You must have something, Nicola. And also wipe the spit off the mikes. (*He runs his hand along the desk.*) And wipe this too, it's filthy.

REX (*coming down from box*). Len — that was . . . that was incredible.

LEONARD (*fast*). Was it? I can do without your comments.

MICK. Yes it was, Mr Brazil — really great.

REX. Yes it was. It really was? It was a knockout. (*Smiles.*) I.ve got Carol and everybody standing by. Everything's waiting.

BIG JOHN *enters.*

LEONARD (*turns*). What are you doing there?

JOHN. Tremendous, Leonard. (*To* REX.) Wasn't it? (*He looks at the girls.*) You OK, girls — bearing up? I've got some News for you now.

LEONARD (*turns*). I wasn't expecting the News, I thought it had moved.

JOHN (*smiling, unaware*). No, same schedule as always. Of course — (*Smiles.*) — life must go on.

Off-stage, one telephone bell starts ringing faintly; it's answered.

REX. There we go. That's the first, they've started!

LEONARD. Get their drinks, Rex.

REX goes.

LEONARD. All right, girls, keep still where you are. Everyone keep still and don't speak. (*He moves to the mike, stops the record.*) And to interrupt there! For believe it or not, Big John is here with the local, national and international news.

BIG JOHN *sits, begins to read the News, at first mundane items.*

(*From the back wall in his strong DJ voice.*) They call this News. (*He looks at* NICOLA.) Waste of time, isn't it. (BIG JOHN *is still reading. Louder.*) Do they call this news?

The telephone bells are growing louder, more numerous. BIG JOHN *starts reading more violent items. Suddenly* LEONARD *moves over to the table, presses a button, music bursts out.*

('*Competition*' *voice.*) This is the Final here. Thank you, Big John, for reading the news for us. Now keep ringing . . . Keep those bells going ting-a-ling-a-ling, ring us, *please*. And while I wait, I'll spin another circle of happiness and pour a little more sugar over the city.

Music continues.

JOHN (*astonished*). I was only half-way through, Leonard.

LEONARD. That was enough News, wasn't it? I haven't spent a whole week whipping up the audience to lose them — let them drift away because of this. (*He picks up the news bulletin.*) It can wait an hour, can't it. (*Loud.*) It's going to, anyway.

JOHN (*picking up the bulletin*). All right then — if that's what you want. (*Smiles.*) If *you* say so, first time that's ever happened. But since it's all going so tremendously — (*Smiles.*) — you can't let much get in your way right this moment, I can see that. Certainly I've never heard you in better form. Never. (*He smiles again.*) Are you going to make a lot out of the announcement of the result then . . . ?

LEONARD (*sharp*). All right John.

REX *enters with the drinks.*

JOHN (*smiles*). He's given me the chop, the News has got the chop for the first time.

REX. Yes, I heard — (*He gives drinks to the* GIRLS.)

JANE. Thank you. (*She tries to drink; it's very hot.*)

JOHN. But worth it just this once I think.

LEONARD (*not unpleasant*). Look, get out of here, John, go on — (JOHN *goes.*)

REX. Very soon now, girls, it'll be all over won't it? Leonard.

LEONARD (*back to him*). Yes?

REX. I wondered — I wondered if . . . *my minute* . . .

LEONARD. Did you? (*He cuts the music.*) Hello again — this is the control room, Competition Week — Leicester, England. Jane and Nicola are a little tense, aren't they, a little pale, but they're smiling bravely. Jane's rose is drooping slightly, Nicola's is bulging —

REX. Leonard . . . my minute . . .

LEONARD. Young Rex is here — calling out to me — he's very eager to have a chance to speak to you. Come here. (*He pulls* REX *forward.*) Here's your chance now, young Rex, how's it going?

REX. Hello — it's cracking along, Leonard, cracking. It's a great contest, isn't it, it's a fabulous contest, we're all agog back there — agog.

LEONARD. Are we. (*Staring at him.*) I see, Rex.

REX (*his voice getting louder, more confident*). The voting's very very close — the phones are jumping and ringing back there —

LEONARD. Jumping and ringing?

REX. Yes, Leonard — like they've got toothache. Want to hear it, folks? Want to hear them ringing folks? (*He bends the mike towards the bells.*)

LEONARD. We're not that posh anymore, are we — ?

REX. No — this is *my* voice now Leonard — this is a Rex-type voice. And I just want to say 'Hello' to the listening millions with it. (*Fast, smiling.*) We really seem to have stirred the whole population, Leonard, like soup, we had callers of all ages back there, all sorts, from nine to ninety, all kinds of voices. The machines are over-loading back there — it's terrifying, it's wonderful.

LEONARD. The machines are so busy back there, they're going to explode.

REX. That's right Leonard. Back there we really need six hands and six feet. (*Grins.*) And six tongues! The girls are looking very happy at the moment, waiting for the result, didn't they do well — put up a great show.

LEONARD. We're making the most of things, aren't we Rex — of our chances.

REX. That's right, Leonard — got to, haven't I. And it's a great feeling up here, a whale of a time — except the tension is killing me — stop the tension Leonard — please . . . stop it, don't leave me, Len, don't leave me! You must stop the tension, it's killing me, my left foot's already gone dead.

LEONARD. You're a bit of a joker, aren't you, Rex. (*Louder.*) A bit of a joker.

REX. That's what we all are, Leonard. (*Imitating* LEONARD'*s voice.*) That's why we're here folks — sitting up here, that's how how we've been made, Leonard, isn't that right.

LEONARD. A bit of an aper, aren't we, Rex?

REX. That's what I am, Leonard.

LEONARD (*smiles*). And no questions asked.

REX. Of course not. No questions! That's all I can do, isn't it. I can't be any different. Play it again, Leonard.

LEONARD (*staring at him*). Play it again Rex. Rex likes the sound of his own voice, doesn't he?

REX. Yes! (*He laughs, standing over the mike.*) I like the sound of my own voice all right. And I'd just like to say to the listening millions, it's intoxicating up here, folks. I'm flying with it, really flying. (*He looks at* LEONARD.) That's what we enjoy, folks, isn't it! No need to fear, Len and Rex are here. (*Sudden change of tone. Exuberant, brilliant.*) And look . . . look at this Leonard — see what's happening — I'm losing a little weight, Leonard, see it's slipping off, it's starting to slip off, getting more now — see, reels and reels of fat are dropping off me onto the floor, they are! That's right, at this very moment, I wish you could see it folks, Rex is losing the fat, it's just fallen off, whole streams of it coming away all over the studio, some's even gone over the controls, look at it Leonard, have you ever seen anything like it — have you — But seriously folks —

LEONARD. All right. That's enough, isn't it? (*He pulls him away from the mike.*) His hand is still gripping the microphone, he has to be torn away. Go and silence those bells — Rex, the girls can't wait any more.

REX (*smiling broadly*). I'll go and silence them right away. (*He calls into the mike.*) Last calls please! (*He goes.*)

LEONARD (*into the mike*). Rex has gone for the result . . . has even dressed like me today, folks. Don't worry, girls, we're there now!

NICOLA. Where do you want me to sit?

LEONARD. Sit here please, Nicola Davies. The girls are sitting by me now, I'm holding their hands, one each. They're sitting very straight very calm. 'They're tough girls you've got there, Brazil, they can take it!' Rex is bringing in the result — smiling proudly; that's a big envelope you're holding, Sound Engineer Rex.

REX. Yes, it is . . . Leonard.

LEONARD (*his tone is very quiet*). It has the word 'Winner' on the front in red ink. I'm opening the envelope, this is the moment we've hoped for — (*He looks at the card.*) And the words on the card are — (*He glances at* NICOLA.) — Jane Harris. (*Booming voice, repeating like a machine, fast.*) Jane Harris is the winner, Jane Harris is the winner, Jane Harris is the winner. Let's have some applause. (*He brings up*

tumultuous applause on tape.) How do you feel, Jane?
(*Applause dies away.)*

JANE (*very quiet*). I feel . . . I feel . . . I feel . . .OK . . .

LEONARD. You must be very happy.

JANE (*quiet*). I am, yes.

LEONARD. How does Nicola feel? No hard feelings, I hope?

NICOLA (*quiet*). I'm OK.

LEONARD. Sound Engineer Rex is now going to take you, Jane,
to where Ross is waiting. OK Rex, take her away.

REX. What? You mean me?

LEONARD (*not looking at him, with papers on desk*). Yes, you.

REX (*quietly, watching him*). You're not really letting me handle
it all, are you?

LEONARD (*matter-of-fact*). Yes. It's what you want, isn't it?

REX. What? You're going to let me take her up — her up there,
and deal with Ross and all that?

LEONARD (*not looking up*). That's right. Go on.

REX (*suddenly loud*). Christ — that's incredible. That's really
incredible! (*He takes* JANE's *hand, pulls her towards the
door.*) Come on, you're coming with me. (*He stops by the
door.*) That's fantastic of you, Leonard. I'm not fired then.

LEONARD (*matter-of-fact*). No it doesn't seem you are. There's
no stopping you, anyway.

REX (*looking at him*). I suppose not. (*Slight smile*). Not now.

LEONARD (*not looking up*). Go on, get out of my sight.

REX (*smile*). Right, Leonard. (*He waits for a moment, then
goes out with* JANE.)

Music in the background, allowing LEONARD *to speak when
he wants to.*

LEONARD. Rex . . . an unimaginative kid, isn't he . . . but
going places! (LEONARD *glances up at* MICK, *who hastily
leaves.* LEONARD *glances towards* NICOLA.) We'll be getting
you a car, I hope, to run you back home. (*He is still pent up,
brings music up slightly, switches onto air, red light on, sings
along to the record. DJ voice, very quiet, very tense.*) Any

moment we'll be switching to Studio A, so wherever you are, whatever you're doing, *don't* go anywhere near the switch-off knob, because any minute now you'll be hearing the voice of Rex spreading out towards you — and just a reminder, the great group are going to Nottingham and Manchester, next Wednesday and next Saturday. (*He brings up the music. NICOLA touches the red lightbulb; LEONARD continues looking towards her.*) Don't touch that, it's hot.

NICOLA. Yeah — it is. (*She takes her hand away, picks up her glass of milk.*)

LEONARD (*red light on again*). I, Leonard Brazil, am taking a break now, a quick *snap*, a brrrreak. (*Calling.*) Come in, Studio A, come in there. Hello — come in Rex with the furry voice, it's all yours then!

REX's VOICE (*on the intercom, booming over the loudspeakers*). Thank you Leonard for that introduction — Rex with the furry voice — there, we all liked that! And I have with me Jane, the lucky winner of the Competition of the Century, and the voice you've all been waiting for, in fact he's sitting in front of me and Jane right now, not only his voice, but *all of him*, the whole of the one and only, the greatest —

LEONARD *clicks it off.*

LEONARD. There.

NICOLA. Yes. (*Silence.*)

LEONARD *gets up, crumples a piece of paper.*

LEONARD. You OK?

NICOLA. Yes. (*She drops the full glass of milk; she hasn't drunk any of it.*)

LEONARD. Don't worry about that — it's a horrible mess in here anyway, isn't it?

NICOLA (*stares round the studio*). Yes.

LEONARD (*beginning to put on his jacket, and get his papers together*). Disgusting leftovers everywhere — the junk that's been sent in here, been pouring in, crammed away in every corner and going bad, probably; it's a nasty room, this, isn't it? (*He rubs at the milk on the floor with his foot.*) This milk'll go grey-blue in a moment, hasn't been cleaned for months in here. (*Loud.*) It doesn't *look like* the nerve-centre of something, does it?! Are you all right? *(He stands ready to go; looks at her.)*

NICOLA. Yes, I'm OK.

LEONARD. Don't worry! We probably couldn't have let you win anyway — could we. Because you won that LP. It wouldn't have looked very good if you'd won both, would it. Might have smelt, as they say. (*Pause.*) So you couldn't really have won.

NICOLA (*quiet, blank*). No . . . I know.

LEONARD. And you've done all right, haven't you, fought your way up into here for the final. You've been quite lucky really . . . (*Pause. Louder as* NICOLA *doesn't react.*) You have, you know.

NICOLA. I know that, yes.

LEONARD. Good. Not much to see in London anyway. You mustn't believe what I've been saying about it, it's dead. (*Pause.*) She's not going in *their* car anyway, she's going in the second car of the convoy with the cook and the luggage. Half an hour's chat at midnight with them in a motorway cafe and that's all she'll get. (*Pause.*) Here — (*He picks up a tape.*) — there's the tape of Ross, we've been playing, you can have it, if you want. (*Then quick change.*) No, I think it's got to be returned, *they* want to use it again. Stop us cutting him up. (*Suddenly loud, changing tone, straight to her.*) You can't really like this shit, can you, do you really, deep down inside, like this music?

She doesn't reply.

Do you!

NICOLA. A bit.

LEONARD. A bit — what does that mean? Either you do or you don't.

NICOLA. Yes, I do.

LEONARD. Right! (*Pause.*) You know, Nicola, if, ten years ago, five years ago even — (*Mock voice.*) — when things were very different, I'd been told that I'd be doing this job, playing this mindless milk chocolate pap or manufactured synthetic violence endlessly to kids like you, I wouldn't have thought it remotely possible. (*Loud.*) Not at all, it's not exactly what

I imagined happening, not even in my greyest moments. It's extraordinary really that things have resulted in *you!* Do you know that?

NICOLA *is in front of him, silent.*

I've been offered a job, too, Nicola, to do some more, a much much bigger job, to chatter and gibber to many more people, lots of them, all waiting for it. And they want a decision. Quick answer.

NICOLA *watches him; he stares straight at her.*

This competition has been a great puller, you'll be pleased to know — the most successful of all, you're the only lucrative corner of the market left, that never fails, do you know that —

NICOLA (*staring straight at him*). Yes.

LEONARD. All you have to do is just stop buying, don't you, as simple as that, just stop, refuse to lap it up any more. Spit it out. *I mean that.* (*Suddenly loud.*) Do you — understand a word I'm saying?

NICOLA. Yes . . . I do.

LEONARD. I don't often meet any of my audience this close. I picked you out, do you know that, homed in on you . . . I picked out that voice, that slightly dead, empty sort of voice. Picked it out as Miss Average — which in fact you probably are not, and I followed that flat voice, each announcement was aimed at it.

NICOLA. Oh I see —

LEONARD. I let it get through each stage, let you clamber up here, because I wanted to see it . . . *meet you*, face you. (*Loud.*) And now you're here.

NICOLA (*quiet*). Yes.

LEONARD (*louder*). Is monosyllables all I'm going to get?

NICOLA. Yes.

LEONARD. What did you think of the Competition, then? (*Pause.*) Come on . . .

NICOLA. I don't know. (*She looks straight at him, cold.*) I don't know what I thought of it . . .

LEONARD (*abrasive*). Got a little out of hand — though it'll have sounded all right down there. Is that how you'd put it?

NICOLA. I don't know.

LEONARD. There was a touch of revenge, don't you think . . . I must want a little revenge . . . I glanced at you before the first question and saw that stare, that blank, infuriatingly vacant gaze, and then it just happened. I wanted to see just how far I *could push you*, how much you'd take — I was hoping you'd come back — that something would come shooting back, that you'd put up a fight Nicola. That you'd explode Nicola, you'd explode. Do you see, why didn't, why don't you . . .? *(Suddenly very loud.)* What's the matter with all you kids now, what is it? Come on, answer me, you know what I'm talking about, you're not a small child, you know what I mean. *(Pause. Abrasive.)* Are you going to talk to me?

NICOLA. No.

LEONARD. Why not?

NICOLA. I . . . *(Slight pause.)* I don't want to.

LEONARD. You don't want to. *(Pause.)* Come here. *(Loud.)* You're not hoping to get away with that, are you? Come here — come on Nicola. *(He pulls her to him, holds her by the arm.)* There — After all, I brought you up here for this meeting — *(He stares down at her — slight smile.)* What are you going to do now, Nicola? *(Pause. She doesn't move.)* You don't even look startled! Nothing!

NICOLA. No.

LEONARD *(really loud)*. COME ON! *(He takes hold of her and shakes her really violently for several seconds.)*

After a pause.

Had no effect on you at all.

NICOLA *(slightly louder)*. No.

LEONARD *(still holding her)*. You almost feel, Nicola Davies — as if you're from another planet, do you know that?

No answer. He turns.

I would give you a lift, love, but I'm going for a walk. Got to work things out. *(Very matter-of-fact.)* What are we going to do, love. *(She looks about her.)* Are you all right? *(He looks*

about the studio.) You won't do anything silly — will you?
No. (*He flicks on the switch:* ROSS's *voice booms out.*)
There! (*He goes.*)

ROSS's VOICE (*on the speakers*). The receptions we've been
getting have been fabulous, *really* fabulous. You know, really
warm, and we've had no bother, no trouble of any kind,
everything's been calm and nice . . .

NICOLA *picks up her bag.*

. . . which should put a sock in all those critics who've written
about us. And to see those faces in the front row, they're
always a special sort of face in the front row. I don't know
how to describe it, but in the front row the faces are always
different.

NICOLA *fastens her bag, moves out of the studio.*

REX's VOICE (*on the speakers*). I know what you mean. I've
noticed that myself.

NICOLA *moves into the shop area.*

ROSS's VOICE (*on the speakers*). And also English front rows
are very different, totally different in a funny kind of way
from American front rows.

ROSS's *voice fades into the noise of the loud hum from the
shop's fridge, as the lights go down on the studio and up on*
SUSAN *in the supermarket . . .*

Scene Three

The supermarket. NICOLA *stands facing* SUSAN, *who is standing
opposite her holding a dustpan and brush. The shop has closed
its doors for the evening. Silent and dark except for the light
shining up from inside the fridge.*

SUSAN (*standing by the fridge*). Why are you so late? . . . I
wondered if you'd show up at all.

NICOLA. I got delayed.

SUSAN. I've been hanging around for a long time. Everybody's
gone, almost. Had to do this corner all by myself, and there
was lots of it, bloody place. Done most of it now anyway.
So you lost, didn't you.

NICOLA. Yes . . . that's right . . . I lost. (*Pause.* NICOLA *smiles slightly.*) You're right. (*She turns, bites her lip. Her mood is of contained violence.*)

SUSAN. You OK?

NICOLA. Yes, I'm OK. (*Louder.*) I'm all right. (*Pause.*) Did you hear it?

SUSAN. Yes, some of it.

NICOLA (*suddenly loud*). What do you mean, *some* of it?

SUSAN (*surprised*). No, I heard it. Quite a lot.

NICOLA (*very loud, savage*). Why didn't you hear all of it? (*Shouts.*) YOU SHOULD HAVE HEARD IT ALL! ALL OF IT! (*Pause, suddenly matter-of-fact.*) You'd only have been able to tell if you'd seen it. Been there. (*Pause.*) What did you think?

SUSAN. You were OK.

NICOLA (*pulls a fish-fingers packet out of the fridge, lets it drop*). OK?

SUSAN. Ought to have won, really.

NICOLA. Yes, I know. (*Pause.*) It was very hot up there.

SUSAN. They really put you through it.

NICOLA. Yeah — they did. (*Sudden smile.*) Hey, look at that. (*She pulls a leg of the dummy out of her bag.*) It fell off! That's what they made me make . . .

SUSAN. That's right. (*Smiles.*) Should do it to it all.

NICOLA *drops the bag with the dummy in it into the fridge. She smiles.*

NICOLA. Could put it in here, watch it go hard, freeze it, then pull it to bits easily. (*She pulls out the bag, stares into the fridge.*) Not much left in there, is there. (*Suddenly louder.*) Not much left!

SUSAN. Yes. (*She is bewildered by* NICOLA's *aggression.*)

NICOLA (*fast*). It was interesting really seeing him, seeing the DJ there, that was interesting! (*Suddenly louder, quite clenched.*) It was all interesting — *everything.* (*She pulls more packets of fish-fingers out of the fridge.*) Lot of these left, anyway.

As they talk, NICOLA *keeps pulling more packets out, undoing packets and dropping them.*

SUSAN. You going to queue for the concert?

NICOLA. Don't think so. I don't want to. They're all right, I s'pose. But I'm not going this time.

SUSAN. I might go. I don't know.

NICOLA. We're too late — *because of this.* Never get a good place in the queue. We'd never get in.

SUSAN (*suddenly relaxing*). No we wouldn't, would we.

NICOLA. Anyway it's not worth it. It really isn't!

She is holding the bag very tight, with the dummy inside; clenched violence inside her.

SUSAN. Are you *all right,* Nicola? Not ill or anything?

NICOLA (*louder*). Yuh, I'm fine. I told you. There's nothing wrong with me. (*She glances behind her.*) It's all different here when it's dark. (*By the fridge again.*) Nobody's watching. We could throw all this out if we wanted. And all the rest, spread all over the shop — first thing they'd see Monday morning. They'd never know who it was.

SUSAN (*excited, uninhibited violence*). We can do the whole place, if we wanted, the cameras are off, dead, it wouldn't take long. The shelves come down easily, just fall off, and the stacks of cans, just have to pull one and millions come down, all pouring down. Could make them all do that. We could finish the whole place. It would be very easy really . . .

NICOLA. Yes. (*Loud.*) TEAR THROUGH IT IF WE WANTED. (*Pause.*) But it's not worth it really. I don't think it's worth it. Maybe next time. We'll see next time. (*Savage.*) I'll see next time.

SUSAN. What do you mean, next time?

NICOLA (*biting her lip*). I don't know, I don't know, do I?

SUSAN. You're in a funny mood, aren't you?

NICOLA (*clenched*). Yeah, that's right. I s'pose I am.

SUSAN. You are — never seen you like this —

NICOLA. No, that's right.

We hear the distant noise of a radio voice.

SUSAN. Sssh — hear that — listen to that.

NICOLA. What?

SUSAN. There — hear it now? That talking, that voice —

NICOLA. Yes.

SUSAN. Where's it coming from — somewhere near — very near. Can't see.

NICOLA. Don't know — but it's him all right.

The girls freeze.

The lights go down on the supermarket and cross fade to the studio . . .

Scene Four

The studio. LEONARD *is standing over controls. He stops his own noise.*

LEONARD (*his tone is quiet, sharp, he takes the speed slowly*). Hello. That was of course LB's jingle, and this is a very special moment, for which I'm standing, I really am, all alone in this studio, standing above the controls, which are hot and steaming. Thank you to Rex for his first great solo over the air. Very smooth, very good. That was a Rex-type interview. (*His tone changes.*) I've got to tell you something now which is quite a big surprise, because today I was offered a very big job in London, with the very splendid Capital Radio — and they offered me a lot of money and a large, large audience, in London, the capital of this fine country of ours, and a fat programme, to do my very own thing. They offered me this job earlier today. 'We must have you,' they said. 'We must have him.' And I have thought about it. (*He smiles; loud, jubilant.*) And I have accepted their offer! Yes I have. I'm going there. I, Len Brazil, Lennnnnn Brazil, am leaving you for Capital Land, London! I hear it'll need four people to fill my job here, which is nice, but I'm going to London where all the action is — where I'll be giving a few jokes and all the hits and more, all the sounds and more, all the luck and more, where I'll be seeing us through our present troubles, obliterating the bad times — that's a Big Word — and remembering the good times, oh yes — and letting people remember and letting them forget. Drowning all our sorrows, yes I said drowning, till we're emerging out of the clouds, of course. And now I hope my voice is reaching out, spreading to the four corners of our area — across the whole city, through the blackness, swooping into cars on the motorway and down chimneys, and through brick walls and across pylons. (*His DJ voice.*) Over the whole domain, until it reaches you. Because I want to say, I'm sorry folks, but there it is. I'm sorry to leave you folks; but it's how I've always wanted to do things of course. (*Smiles to himself.*) What I wanted! Don't spit on the animals. I'm speaking to *you* now, I am, remember this, when you're in London, don't forget to give us a ring, want to hear from you, over the air, at the very least don't forget to tune in. Yes tune in! What are you doing Brazil — tell us — what on earth is he doing — He's saying *Goodbye* and *don't forget.* We're going to lick it, of course we will. No need to worry, no need to be sad. Shout that out. So tune in, I said tune in. Because I'll take your mind off things, oh yes. I will. (*He brings the music in louder.*) Hear that — some music! Music for Len's farewell. Tune in, I said. (*Very loud.*) TUNE IN. This is how we like it. I've got some great times for you, oh yes. You know I'll never let you down. That was Competition week. This is Len Brazil. Be seeing you.

Fade.

YELLOW BLUES
Slowly

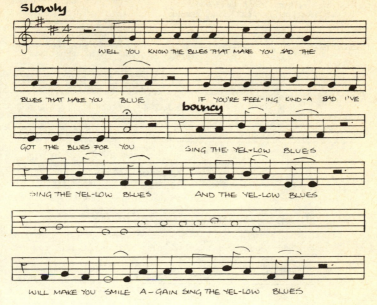

WELL YOU KNOW THE BLUES THAT MAKE YOU SAD THE

BLUES THAT MAKE YOU BLUE IF YOU'RE FEEL-ING KIND-A BAD I'VE

bouncy

GOT THE BLUES FOR YOU SING THE YEL-LOW BLUES

SING THE YEL-LOW BLUES AND THE YEL-LOW BLUES

WILL MAKE YOU SMILE A-GAIN SING THE YEL-LOW BLUES

I CAN GIVE YOU LOVE
slow ballad – lilting beat

I'LL GIVE YOU AP-RIL SHOW-ERS DAFF-O-DILS IN MA-

-Y I'LL GIVE YOU JUNE-TIME FLOW-ERS RO-SES EV-ERY DA-

-Y DON'T YOU THINK THAT MA-Y-BE YOU COULD BE MY

BA — BY MY SWEET LIT-TLE ANG-EL FROM A-BOVE 'CAUSE I CAN GIVE YOU

LOVE*(YES I CAN) I CAN GIVE YOU LOVE*(BE YOUR MAN) BE MY LIT-TLE

BA-BY DON'T YOU THINK THAT MAY-BE I CAN GIVE YOU LOVE

I LOVED YOU IN DEC-EM-BER — — -

*(These lines are sung by another singer on the record at the
beginning of Act Two. but not by JANE in the competition.
She leaves a pause, and beats time nervously with her foot.)